Our Hearts' True Home

Fourteen warm, inspiring stories of women
discovering the ancient Christian Faith

edited by Virginia Nieuwsma

CONCILIAR PRESS
Ben Lomond, California

OUR HEARTS' TRUE HOME
© 1996 Conciliar Press
Ben Lomond, California

ISBN 1-888212-02-0
All rights reserved
Printed in Canada

Conciliar Press
P.O. Box 76, Ben Lomond, California 95005-0076

Library of Congress Cataloging in Publication Data

Our hearts' true home : fourteen warm, inspiring stories of women
    discovering the ancient Christian faith / edited by Virginia
    Nieuwsma.
        p. cm.
    Includes bibliographical references.
    ISBN 1-888212-02-0

1. Women in the Orthodox Eastern Church -- United States --
    Biography. 2. Orthodox Eastern converts -- United States --
    Biography. 3. Orthodox Eastern Church -- United States --
    Membership. I. Nieuwsma, Virginia, 1959–

BX342.5.097   1996
281.9'092'273--dc20
[B]   96-26042
                                                          CIP

To my beloved father and mother,
John and Donna Hubbard,
who have taught me, in word and example,
to follow Christ and His Truth,
regardless of the cost or consequence.
God grant you many years!

Table of Contents

Acknowledgments

Editing this book has been a great joy, more so because of the people who helped pull it together: Deacon Ray Zell and the folks at Conciliar Press; Ginny Silva, who helped me with her editing skills; Mark Mellis, my long-suffering computer expert; the gracious, cooperative women who wrote for this book (and those who wrote manuscripts which couldn't be included); Denise Timby, Kathy Johnstone, Carolyn Murphy, and Erin Coffin, who cooked for me, watched my kids, and gave me the gift of a silent house; Fathers Jon Braun, Seraphim Bell, and Patrick Jackson, whose spiritual guidance has nurtured and stretched me; and finally, my five greatest blessings from God—Tim, my unfailing encourager and the one I can thank for this precious Church, Annie—sensitive helper and extraordinary manager, April—sunny cheerleader and kiddy-watcher, Allison—giver of heartfelt affection and table-setter, and Teddy—comedian and ball player.

Foreword

Tonight I went to church. But first, my day held its usual round of shopping, stopping by the bank, taking the kids to music lessons, tidying the house. Seeing I was going to be late for the Liturgy, I rushed through some hasty instructions for my oldest daughter, who was helping the younger children with dinner. But even as I walked up to our St. Stephen Church, the sweet melodies and smells escaped through the door and I began to refocus. Entering, I noticed the icon for the Feast of the Meeting of Christ in the Temple, posted by the door. Now I was entering Church time, eternal time, and everywhere I looked reminded me of this. As the candles cast a soft glow, I marveled that the Giver of the Law chose to become subject to the Law, when His mother presented Him to Simeon and Anna. Again I savored the mystery of the Incarnation, made ever-fresh by the hymns and the Scriptures of the Church. I listened to prophecies of this Savior from Isaiah. If my attention wandered, I looked at the icons of St. Patrick, who converted an entire nation, and St. Mary of Egypt, who repented of her sins for forty years in the desert. Most glorious and mysterious of all, I came forward at the Liturgy's conclusion to receive His very life in the Eucharist. Those of us at this banquet properly responded—"Lord, have mercy!" and "Alleluia!"

Driving home, I was still living in this heavenly realm; yet nothing around me had changed. In one of many paradoxes, I find that the longer I'm an Orthodox Christian, the more I yearn for the presence of the Holy Spirit in the Church's worship, and yet when I "go forth in peace, in the name of the Lord" I am also able to live with greater joy.

Orthodox services *are* other-worldly—that's the point! We are worshipping the almighty God, after all. But in so doing we not only prepare for—and in a very real sense, enter into—heaven, we also are fed and sustained, more equipped to live in this world as well. The truth is, God isn't as concerned with changing our circumstances as He is with changing us. St. Seraphim of Sarov said, "Obtain peace, and thousands around you will find salvation."

Even as I turned the key to my home's front door, I sensed that the peace of the heavenly worship was still with me. The food smelled a little better, I felt a little more warmth as I greeted my children, the clutter I left didn't seem as annoying.

A simple illustration, maybe, but this is life in the Church: arming us for the here and now—and yet always permeated with that beautiful heavenly fragrance and flavor, so that we never forget our eventual destiny. Isn't this full-orbed worship what our souls were created for, what we all long for?

The fifteen women whose stories make up this book have found this in Orthodoxy, and they earnestly desire to communicate what it has meant for them. Through their lives they have faced many challenges, some more daunting than you or I may ever know. But though they are different ages, come from many backgrounds, and work at varied professions, they all discovered one thing: Christian faith and practice, as it is meant to be believed and lived, can only be found in its fullness in the Holy Orthodox Church.

Orthodoxy has been called the best-kept secret in America. The women of this book earnestly hope and pray, for your sakes and that of future generations, that this does not remain so. We have no desire to hoard this treasure, but earnestly long for our friends and neighbors, at whatever point they find themselves on their spiritual journeys, to inherit this gold mine for themselves and their families. God grant you great wisdom, discernment, and His still small voice as you read this book and try to decide for yourself whether this Orthodox Church has a claim on you.

Virginia Nieuwsma
February 2, 1996

Frederica Mathewes-Green

In the Passenger's Seat

He was an Episcopal priest, but he was standing in an Orthodox church on this Saturday night and thinking about Truth. At the altar a gold-robed priest strode back and forth swinging incense, moving in and out of the doors of the iconostasis according to a pattern that was as yet unfamiliar. Golden bells chimed against the censer, and the light was smoky and dim. Over to the left a small choir was singing in haunting harmony, voices twining in *a cappella* simplicity. The Truth part was this: the ancient words of this vesperal service had been chanted for more than a millennium. *Lex orandi, lex credendi* ("what you pray, you believe"). This was a church that had never, could never, apostatize.

She was his wife, and she was standing next to him thinking about her feet. They hurt. She wondered why they had pews if you had to stand up all the time. The struggling choir was weak and singing in an unintelligible language that may have been English. The few other worshippers weren't participating in the service in any visible way. Why did they hide the altar behind

11

a wall? It was annoying how the priest kept popping in and out of the doors like a figure on a Swiss clock. The service dragged on following no discernible pattern, and it was interminable. Once the priest had said, "Let us complete our evening prayer to the Lord." She checked her watch again; that was ten minutes ago, and still no end in sight.

As I ponder my move from the Episcopal Church to Eastern Orthodoxy, I realize that I didn't make the trip alone, but in a two-seater. And I wasn't the one in the driver's seat.

This is more relevant than may initially appear. Something about Eastern Orthodoxy has immense appeal to men, and it's something that their wives are generally slower to get. The appeal of joining this vast, ancient, rock-solid communion must be something like the appeal of joining the Marines. It's going to demand everything out of you, and it's not going to cater to your individual whims, but when it's through with you you're going to be more than you ever knew you could be. It's going to demand, not death on the battlefield, but death to self in a million painful ways, and God is going to be sovereign. It's a guy thing. You wouldn't understand.

When I asked members of our little mission, "Why did you become a member?" two women (both enthusiastic converts now) used the same words: "My husband dragged me here kicking and screaming." Several others each echoed that it had been her husband's idea—he'd been swept off his feet and brought her along willy-nilly. Another woman told how she left inquirers' class each week vowing never to go again, only to have her husband wheedle her into giving it one more try; this lasted right up to the day of her chrismation. I can imagine how her husband looked, because that's how Gary looked: blissful, cautious, eager, and with a certain cat-who-ate-the-canary, you'll-find-out smile.

That night at Vespers a few years ago I was one of those balky wives. Gary and I stood side by side feeling radically different things, but the pattern could have been predicted from the beginning. When we first met over twenty years ago, he was a political animal who just didn't think much about God; I was a passionate agnostic, angry at God for not existing, eagerly attacking the faith of Christian friends.

Gary's shell began to crack when a professor required the class to read a Gospel, and he chose Mark "because it's the shortest." I can remember the sense of foreboding I felt when he said, "There's something about this Jesus. He speaks with authority. I've never encountered anything like it before in my life. If Jesus says there's a God, there must be one."

I read a Hindu prayer at our wedding, then we left for a hitchhiker's tour of Europe. On June 20, 1974, I walked into a church in Dublin, took one look at a statue of Jesus, and found myself on my knees. I could hear an interior presence saying, "I am your life," and I

13

knew it was the One I had rejected and ridiculed, come at last to seize me forever. It was a shattering experience from which I emerged blinking like a newborn, and decades later I still feel overwhelming awe and gratitude for that rescue, that vast and undeserved gift. It's like the story of the farmer who had to whack his donkey with a two-by-four to get its attention. I imagine that, when God needs a two-by-four that big, He must be dealing with a pretty big donkey.

True to form, Gary needed Truth, while I needed a personal, mystical experience. In the years that followed we went to Episcopal seminary together, were "baptized in the Holy Spirit" together, and spent several years in the early charismatic movement. He was ordained a priest and we moved to a new church every few years, having babies along the way. When the charismatic experience grew stale, he rediscovered the high liturgical tradition of his childhood, while I went into spiritual direction and centering prayer. Though there are pitfalls along each of these paths—high-churchiness can devolve into form-but-not-substance, mysticism can float into new-age self-centeredness—neither of us lost our central commitment to Jesus as Lord. Wherever we went, God kept us near Himself and each other.

As I shifted my aching feet on the floor of that dingy Orthodox church, I wondered whether Gary's new direction would ever make sense to me. What had pushed him in the door of this church in the first place was growing unease with changes in the Episcopal Church, changes both moral and theological.

For example, Bishop Jack Spong had brought national attention to his New Jersey diocese; he seemed to interpret the Anglican fondness for the *via media* ("the middle way") as "the way of the media." Spong pronounced that the gender of sex partners was unimportant as long as they were in a monogamous relationship, and began ordaining gays in defiance of national church consensus.

But lines drawn in the sand are easily redrawn further south. One ordinand, Robert Williams, declared that monogamy was unnecessary, and Mother Teresa's life would be "significantly enhanced . . . if she got laid." Spong could fire Williams from his ministry, but could not un-ordain him; there was a lesson here apparent to everyone but Bishop Spong.

If those events outraged us, others left us feeling frustrated and sad. In July of 1991, I was present for a vote of the Episcopal House of Bishops, a resolution requiring ordained clergy to abstain from sex outside of marriage. When the ballots were counted, the resolution had failed. I remember thinking, "This isn't a church anymore; it has no intention of following its Lord."

Meanwhile, it became fashionable to doubt Jesus' miracles, the Virgin Birth, even the bodily Resurrection. Before his consecration as England's fourth-highest-ranking cleric, David Jenkins claimed that miracles were in the eye of the beholder. Of Jesus' physical

Resurrection he sniffed, "I'm bothered about what I call 'God and conjuring tricks.'" He was consecrated Bishop of Durham on July 6, 1984; two nights later, lightning struck from a cloudless sky and burnt down a wing of the cathedral. Beholders thought they might have seen a miracle.

Home in Baltimore, such shenanigans were wearing on my husband. He banded together with five other "troublesome priests" and wrote a document asserting seven points of theological orthodoxy. They called it the Baltimore Declaration. It prompted a minor dust storm, but the national church lumbered on its way as undisturbed as a water buffalo by a mosquito.

Gary at last decided he could no longer be under the authority of apostate bishops; he had to be in the line of Truth. But where to go? He briefly considered the "continuing" Anglican churches, but felt that move would take him even further from the One, Holy, Catholic, and Apostolic Church. Also, he began to believe that the compromising flaw lay at the very heart of Anglicanism. The beloved doctrine of "comprehensiveness" suggested, "Let's share the same prayers, the same words about the faith, but they can mean different things to you than to me." Not a common faith, but common *words* about the faith—mere flimsy words. A church at peace can survive this way; a church attacked by pleading heresies must tumble into accommodation, reducing orthodoxy to shreds.

Roman Catholicism was the next obvious choice, and we looked into the Pastoral Provision whereby married Episcopal priests become married Catholic priests. But, ironically, pro-Provision literature gave us serious doubts. A book titled *Married to a Catholic Priest* painted an unintentionally grim picture: would we be told to sell our furniture, live in a furnished apartment, never be allowed to retire, ordered to teach high school instead of pastor, and be fourth on a huge staff, under supervision of a hostile feminist nun? Despite that author's cheery "it was worth it all," it wouldn't be worth it all to me.

Then there was the matter of theology. We remained worried by traces of salvation-by-works in Catholic theology. In fact, Catholic theology seemed in general too overdone, compelled to parse every sentience and split every infinitude. I call it "driving nails with your forehead."

Gary was invited to join a small group of Protestant clergy for an evening with Orthodox evangelist Father Peter Gillquist, and went carrying some hard questions; Father Peter later said he thought Gary was the one who would never convert. But the questions were evidence of urgent wrestling. Father Peter directed Gary to the commentaries of St. John Chrysostom, who firmly upheld salvation by faith. In a sermon on 1 Timothy, for example, Chrysostom says that the best purpose of the law is to reveal that it cannot save us; it then "remits us to Him who can do so."

Then I re-encountered a history lesson that had

eluded me in seminary, but now took on vital importance. For the first thousand years, the thread of Christian unity was preserved worldwide through battering waves of heresies. The method was collegial, not authoritarian; disputes were settled in Church Councils, whose decisions were not valid unless received by the whole community. The Faith was indeed common: what was believed by all people, in all times, in all places. The degree of unity won this way was amazing. Though there was some local liturgical variation, the Church was strikingly uniform in faith and practice across vast distances, and at a time when communication was far from easy. This unity was so consistent that I could attribute it to nothing but the Holy Spirit.

Then a developing split between East and West broke open. The Church had five centers: Jerusalem, Antioch, Alexandria, Constantinople, and Rome. The bishop of Rome was accorded special honorary, but not authoritative, status. But by the eleventh century, the papacy was seeking expanded power over the worldwide church. The pope wished, for example, to add the word *filioque* ("and the Son") to the Nicene Creed, which had been in common use since A.D. 325. While this controversy sounds at first picayune, it changes the Trinity from—visually speaking—a triangle with God the Father at the top, to one tipped over, both Father and Son above the Holy Spirit.

The other four patriarchs objected that the Holy Spirit would not have waited a thousand years to clarify the role of the bishop of Rome, and that a Church Council would be necessary to amend the Creed. The conflict grew worse, and the legate of the pope excommunicated the patriarch of Constantinople on Christmas Day of the year 1054.

When West severed from East in this one-to-four split, the Orthodox churches continued united, as they have to the present day (Russian Orthodox, Greek Orthodox, and so forth are just national expressions of the same worldwide Church). Unlike the Western church, the Church of the East went through Christianity's second millennium without being shattered into fragments by theological disputes. This is despite horrific persecution and martyrdom: twenty million Russian Orthodox are estimated to have been martyred in this century alone.

When Rome was set free to create new doctrines, it went on adding to the Faith; when the Reformation showed up five hundred years later, it was spurred by a desire to whittle back to the original. But the Reformers had only the Bible to guide them, which sincere people can interpret in wildly different ways, as shown by the nearly 2500 different Protestant "Bible-based" groups. Like untrained gardeners going into an overgrown yard, the Reformers hacked about with machetes, slashing unknowingly through material that had been affirmed for the first thousand years of Christianity: the sacraments, the honoring of Mary, the eucharistic Real Presence. Protestants were trying to rediscover the ancient Church, but instead they created a dancing array of Sorcerer's Apprentice brooms, all trying to sweep the Faith clean.

These doctrinal conflicts contributed to a Western tendency to make faith more *assensus* than *fiducia*, more ideas about God than surrender to Him. The Orthodox Church, escaping this discord, could admire a butterfly without having to pin its head to a board. For example, rather than over-defining Jesus' presence in the Eucharist, or tossing the concept out entirely, Orthodox are content to say that the bread and wine become His Body and Blood simply because they "change." In Orthodox theology there is a humility, a willingness to let mystery remain beyond comprehension.

The stance of an Orthodox believer is similarly humble and childlike: we are sinners, receiving the overwhelming love of God, and we stand before Him in gratitude. This is, I think, one of the reasons we kiss so much—we kiss icons, the Gospel book, the Cross, and each other. On Sunday we use the Liturgy of St. John Chrysostom (A.D. 347-407), and thank God for sending His Son "into the world to save sinners, of whom I am chief." Grateful repentance is such a constant in Orthodox worship that New Agers attracted by the mystical smells and bells find they can't take more than a couple of weeks—not without conversion.

I paint here in hindsight a rushing tide of conviction about the Truth of Orthodoxy which swept my husband away. At the time, I was having none of it.

Orthodoxy was too foreign, too old, too fancy. I didn't care what they said, I just couldn't believe that this was what the worship of the early Church looked like—all the cluttered doodads of gold, incense, and fancy vestments. My vague assumption was that early Christians just sat around on the floor, probably in their blue jeans, talking about what a great guy Jesus was. It was embarrassing to review Scripture and realize that, from Exodus to Revelation, worship is clothed in gold, silver, precious stones, embroidery, robes of gorgeous fabric, bells, and candles; I don't know of an instance of scriptural worship that doesn't include incense. God ordered beauty, even extravagant beauty, in worship even while His people were still wandering the desert and living in tents. Beauty must mean something that no-nonsense, head-driven Christians fail to grasp.

Unfortunately, the revised Roman Catholic mass has too often lost its beauty; instead, it has the earnest, vacant feeling of seventies smiley-face pop culture. Protestant churches, on the other hand, usually look like classrooms, and what happens there is more likely to be teaching than worship. When I visit one for a morning of great music, powerful preaching, and warm fellowship, I leave thinking, "Gee, maybe they come back later to do the worship part." If scriptural worship is any guide, these Sunday-morning exercises are missing something.

Gary was rarin' to go, but I put on the brakes. Oddly, I wasn't concerned about finances, even though becoming Orthodox meant throwing away a fifteen-year career when our three kids were entering their teens. Nor did I feel loyal affection for the Episcopal Church, either nationally or in our little parish, where, as a pro-life activist, I felt lonely and rejected. But I was afraid we would be leaving for the wrong reason: because we weren't happy. Too many people leave marriages, abort children, or betray other commitments because they feel insufficiently fulfilled. Besides, even if the Episcopal Church was lost to apostasy, didn't God need chaplains on the Titanic? Hadn't we better stay where He planted us?

But Gary's dedication to Truth was stronger than my hesitation, and I finally agreed to go along. On January 30, 1993, I found myself standing before Bishop ANTOUN as he anointed me with holy oil, calling out, "The seal of the gift of the Holy Spirit!" "Seal!" the congregation shouted. Five other families came with us from our Episcopal parish that day, and two weeks later we celebrated our first Liturgy, at a homemade altar, in a borrowed space, with borrowed appointments. Three years later, Holy Cross Mission numbers forty families—nearly all converts.

A continent away, someone I've met only by mail is writing me a letter. She's a multi-generation evangelical, descended from missionaries and professors at Christian colleges. Now her husband has begun looking into Orthodoxy and shows the signs, so familiar to me, of beginning that plummeting dive. Her words are familiar, too:

> "This is a church whose disciplines and life, I feel, appeal initially more to men. To me it all seems so . . . hard. In my spiritual walk up to this point my heart has led my head. I might go to church mad and unrepentant, but with a worship chorus in a lilting tune, or a heartfelt spontaneous prayer, my heart would begin to soften. I'd come out ready to live the obedient life.
>
> "Orthodoxy makes sense in my head, but I yearn for something to grab my gut and help me over the hump labeled 'self.' All the 'soft' music, etc., that used to draw me is missing and I'm left in this massive struggle with my will. Does that make sense? Doesn't a spoonful of sugar help the medicine go down, and all that?
>
> "And how do women eventually come to terms with this somewhat austere church?"

How did I?

Now I can't imagine ever not being Orthodox. Here is my home, my joy, my fulfillment; I tasted and saw, and nothing can compare. But how did I get past the bare-Truth part, the aching-feet part, to discover the rich, mystical beauty of Orthodoxy?

A kaleidoscope of images flashes through my mind.

The textures, the scents, the music of the Liturgy, a continuous song of worship that lifts me every week. The Great Fast of Lent, a discipline far more demanding than I'd ever faced in my Christian walk. Kneeling on Great and Holy Thursday and listening to the hammer blows resound as my husband nailed the icon of Jesus' body to the Cross; seeing my daughter's shoulders shake with sobbing. Easter morning giddiness and champagne at sunrise. Hearing my son say that, after a year of the Divine Liturgy, he didn't like the sentimental hymns of the last three hundred years any more: "They make me feel farther from God." Seeing icons change from something that looks grim and forbidding to something that looks challenging, strong, and true. True.

Truth turns into Beauty in unexpected ways. What was strange and perplexing has become my sweetest home. As I look over my shoulder, I can see this friend not far behind me on the road, and by now it's a familiar sight. Her husband is driving, and she's in the passenger's seat.

Frederica does not expect her daughter will have a Hindu prayer at her wedding, now that her husband Gary (now Father Gregory) is an Orthodox priest! An accomplished writer and editor, Frederica is anticipating the release of her second book, detailing a year in the life of Holy Cross Mission. Frederica sometimes shows up on television and radio as well, as a spokesperson for the pro-life organizations she represents.

∞ Krista West

Whatsoever Things Are Lovely

I began working with my hands at an early age. My father is a machinist by trade and a great handyman. The story is told in my family that when I was three years old, a friend gave me a toy worktable in which plastic "nails" were hammered. I soon tired of this and had to be given a real block of wood along with real hammer and nails. I pounded contentedly until there was literally no space left for a single nail.

I quickly moved on to finer work. My mother taught me to crochet at age five, and sewing and embroidery soon followed. I enjoyed natural talent in these areas and was never happier than when engrossed in some project of my own design.

The only thing I loved as much as using my hands was reading. Stories of any kind were my preference, so long as they were grand and beautiful. These stories helped foster a vivid imagination. I was always inventing situations and characters for my playmates and myself to act out. Occasionally my imagination got me into trouble—I would create fantastic tales about myself and then tell them to my credulous playmates.

It was not that I failed to understand the difference between the real and the imaginary. It was that I preferred the imaginary—not because I wished to escape, but because I longed for resurrection and redemption. I wanted life to be good and beautiful and epic. I sought meaning in everything, and instinctively felt that the stories were so much more real, so much more true, than the ho-hum, day-to-day life I saw in my middle-class world. I wanted every blade of grass, every rock, every person to have a purpose in the grand scheme of things.

Though I remember this sense of mystery and transcendence from an early age, I did not get it from going to church. My non-practicing Lutheran mother and lapsed Roman Catholic father had me baptized as an infant in the Lutheran Church, but religion was never discussed in my family. I grew up having no notion of what I was expected to believe about God. No one told me that He was merciful or loving or awesome, yet somehow I knew these things in my heart anyway. I believed that I could talk to God (I had not been informed otherwise!), and so I assumed that a relationship existed between God and myself.

These ideas were really the beginning of my journey to Orthodoxy. Years later, a school friend introduced me to a local Plymouth Brethren church and my mother and I started attending. Because of this, I was able to convince my parents to send me to a small, evangelical Protestant private school where some of my friends were enrolled.

Though I spent about six years in the Plymouth Brethren church and all of my high school years at this school, I never took root in the evangelical church. I certainly tried, but as time went on, I realized that everyone else's God and my God were not quite the same. I equated God with beauty, not knowing at first that this was seen as idolatry and heresy by many of my brothers and sisters. I loved ritual and order, and increasingly found these things when working with my hands or writing poetry. On one or two occasions I tried to express these still-forming ideas, and quickly learned to keep them to myself. The Christians I knew did not have open minds about such matters, and some even flatly told me that I was wrong.

Never very articulate about my ideas, I sometimes even wondered whether I was mistaken, and yet deep down I believed that somehow, these things had to be true—or else I could not be a Christian. For a time, I even developed an interest in Judaism, reading most of Chaim Potok's novels as well as some Jewish folktales, drawn by the ritual and tradition. These stories appealed to me greatly, but at the time I did not realize that a person could convert to Judaism, so I did not pursue it further.

I met my future husband in my sophomore year of high school, and we became fast friends. I was able to express my ideas with Alban, and I felt relief that I had someone with whom I could discuss God and religion. We began attending a very small community church that had been started by friends of our high school English teacher. The church was beginning to incorporate some semblance of liturgy in worship, and we both enjoyed attending there.

We were married at the end of my senior year in high school (Alban's first year in college). My new husband was studying classics, a natural outgrowth of his love of history and language, and he began reading about the early Church. His readings provided him with new insights into Christianity's roots, and he became curious to find an "apostolic" church. Increasingly uncomfortable in the community church, I supported him, and so we began searching for a place that reflected our changing perspective. Our hunt brought us to a few local parishes of the Episcopal Church, none of which seemed right.

Our fourth Sunday, we visited the local Anglo-Catholic parish. It was a beautiful basilica, and when we went inside—what wonders! The stained glass, the dark wood pews, the marble rood screen, the vestments, the glorious prayers and hymns, the order and structure—it all seemed too good to be true! We were both delighted with our discovery, I for the beauty and majesty, and Alban for the service, which looked to him as if it were straight out of a history book. Neither of us had known that things like this existed. We soon enrolled in confirmation classes, and after completing those became very involved in the parish. Alban began leading Evening Prayer and serving at the altar; I joined the altar guild and began to work on small projects, restoring vestments and liturgical furnishings.

Eventually, the greater problems of the Episcopal Church in the U.S.A. began to affect our little island of Anglo-Catholicism. This was a very sad time for me because I saw heresy and schism affect every member of our small community. The people in our parish knew that we had to make some sort of move out of the Episcopal Church, but we could not agree on how to do it, or where to go.

Alban and I aligned ourselves with a group of people who wanted to move the parish into the Antiochian Orthodox Archdiocese (all Orthodox share the same faith but come from diverse ethnic backgrounds—this jurisdiction is under the Patriarchate of Antioch, located in Damascus). We began to read, Alban extensively and I a little, about Orthodoxy. Our love for the Episcopal Church had long since begun to pale due to that church's increasingly questionable theology, and the way it seemed to blow with the winds of society.

We began to look at the unchanging stability of Orthodoxy with longing eyes. Knowing by this time that we would spend our lives devoted to the Church, most likely with Alban in the priesthood, we yearned for a communion that would not change its doctrines and essential practices. We became part of the core group in the parish that was pro-Orthodoxy, and spent a year trying to educate our fellow parishioners. After a time, we realized that we were no closer to moving our parish into Orthodoxy than when we began, and it was time for us to go. We decided to make our first visit to an Orthodox church, St. George Antiochian Orthodox Church of Portland, Oregon.

My intellectual and emotional conversion to Orthodoxy was finalized the first time I walked down the aisle of St. George's at the beginning of the service. The church building was very humble compared to our gorgeous Anglican basilica, but that day it was as beautiful to me as the fields of heaven. As I walked, I knew that I had found the house of God, that here was where my God resided, and was not only "my" God, but everyone's God. Here was where beauty and creativity and joy had their abode. I heard the censer bells ringing and the voices of the chanter and choir and knew I was home. For good.

After this we signed up for chrismation classes, but I really would have been happy for the priest just to say, "Please sign on the dotted line to become Orthodox." I would have done it, in a heartbeat! Chrismation classes were joy upon joy for me, for I heard God being spoken of in the way that I had always thought of Him. When the priest explained the concept of hell as our own refusal to be in the presence of God, I interrupted the class, and asked him if that was really what the

Orthodox Church taught. I simply could not believe that my own thoughts and musings on the next life were contained in the Church too!

I also learned that the Church takes Christ's Incarnation and Resurrection very seriously, and that they affect each Christian's life every hour, every minute, every second—not just at Christmas or during Holy Week and Pascha (Easter). The way in which the Incarnation and Resurrection stood as a backdrop for Orthodox life fascinated me (and continues to do so), because it was my old idea that everything has meaning and purpose—but in a much greater, holier way than I had ever imagined. Truly, every blade of grass, every rock, every person is redeemed through Christ's Incarnation and Resurrection.

In January, 1993, Alban and I were chrismated at St. George's with eight other people from our former Episcopal parish. St. George's is a strongly Syrian and Lebanese parish, and we loved it. I found the Middle Eastern ethos very comfortable, and I soon preferred the Byzantine Rite to the rite of the Episcopal Church. The community of St. George was extremely welcoming to my husband and me, as well as to the other people who converted with us. There was a wonderful sense of "give and take" in our parish as those of us who had converted learned about a culture that has embraced Orthodox Christianity for two thousand years. In turn, those who had been Orthodox their entire lives saw the riches of their Church anew through the eyes of their convert friends. There were many good conversations (and, of course, many good meals!), and my husband and I were blessed with friendships that will last our entire lives.

Not long after we had found our home in Orthodoxy, we began the application process for seminary. We never even had to question how we would spend our lives. They were centered around the Church and there was nothing else that was equally important. The priesthood quite naturally seemed the life for us. We had discovered so much love and joy in Orthodoxy, there was no struggle over our decision to spend the rest of our lives devoted to the greatest treasure we possessed, our Church.

At the time of this writing, my husband is in his second year of seminary. We are very happy to be pursuing our life goal together, and we both feel blessed to have a work ahead of us that is meaningful and rewarding. I am still very involved in fine handcrafts and I continue to find a path to God through them. I have embarked on some embroidery for vestments and would eventually like to try my hand at embroidered icons. I have a particular interest in the liturgical furnishings of the Orthodox Church and am slowly building my fund of knowledge about their making and care.

While I know some women wrestle greatly with their decisions to convert to Orthodoxy, it was never difficult for me, because the Church embraced and nourished those very "Orthodox" ideas about God that had been growing in my heart since childhood, and she provided a place for me to continue working out my salvation. I am not an intellectual or a theologian, but a simple woman who sits in the pew and offers to God what she can.

Some days, I go to church and halfway through the service, I find that I am paying more attention to the way the tassels are sewn onto the altar covering than to what is going on around me. At first, I would reprimand myself and try to pay closer attention. But now, I find peace in the knowledge that God knows that the altar covering or icon or carving on the iconostasis is just as prayerful for me as the words of the Liturgy are for the next person. "Finally, brethren, whatever things are true, whatever things are noble, whatever things are just, whatever things are pure, whatever things are lovely, whatever things are of good report, if there is any virtue and if there is anything praiseworthy—meditate on these things" (Philippians 4:8).

Krista West now sews cassocks and vestments part-time, putting her love for handcrafts to its highest use. She and her husband Alban are looking forward to serving their first parish after he finishes his degree at Holy Cross Greek Orthodox School of Theology in Brookline, Massachusetts.

∽ Yuen-tsu Yu Velicer

A Foreigner Finds Home

Taipei, Taiwan, is a long way from Michigan, where I came in 1988 to enter a microbiology doctoral program at Michigan State University. Since graduating in 1993, I have been a postdoctoral fellow at the University of Michigan in Ann Arbor. While in the United States, I have undergone many remarkable changes, including beginning to know Jesus Christ, joining the Orthodox Church, marrying an American, and becoming pregnant with our first child.

Our family religious heritage is Buddhism, which was passed on faithfully by my parents as part of our cultural upbringing. (My father works in our family-owned land development business, and my mother was a devoted housewife; she has recently begun hosting a radio show discussing issues of concern to the people of Taipei.) Buddhists believe that anyone can become a 'buddha' or 'enlightened one' through detachment from this world, mystical meditation, and good works. We also held to the idea of reincarnation, which teaches that one's spirit undergoes cyclical incarnations in different bodies (not necessarily human) at different times, with each life's level determined by one's moral performance in the previous life. A good dog could become a human, and a good human might finally break the cycle to enter the bliss of Nirvana, oneness with all. Gautama Buddha, or Buddha, of ancient India is considered the prime example of spiritual life.

As children, we experienced more of external Buddhist rites than of philosophical teachings, though such doctrine was not entirely absent. We honored our ancestors by remembering their days of death or burial, celebrated Buddha's birthday, burned incense at our family altar to secure the protection of our ancestors, offered food to patron buddhas at the local temple, and burned paper money to provide for our ancestors and ward off evil spirits.

Though these traditions were familiar and natural to me, as I grew older Buddhism failed to gain my allegiance as a complete way of life. As a child I didn't think much about religion, but nonetheless found myself praying to an unknown spirit and imagining myself to be a daughter of the moon.

For junior high school I was sent by my parents to a Christian girls' boarding school—not to make me a Christian, but rather a disciplined, well-mannered young lady, better educated than those in the public schools. I attended the best girls' senior high school in Taipei, and later National Taiwan University, where I studied zoology. Obviously, academic performance was emphasized throughout my life, and as an undergraduate I decided to pursue a scientific research career.

On the surface, my journey to Orthodoxy may appear accidental. However, I can now see God's gentle guidance of my paths, though I didn't always recognize that it was He. For many years, I was preoccupied with educational competitiveness and did not think extensively about religion or basic questions such as 'Who am I?'; yet I knew that at some point in life I would need to address such things.

At the Christian boarding school there had been weekly assemblies where guest speakers would tell their conversion stories. The prominence of suffering in many of these stories made me think that Christianity was merely a comfort system for troubled people, and I thought I did not need such a comfort, thank you. Also, the arguments and controversies that arose whenever people discussed religion bothered me and left a bad impression. Though I didn't imagine I would ever become Christian, I did not consider myself an atheist; I just didn't know who had the real God.

My unsettled world-view took a step toward focus when I met Gregory Velicer, a graduate student in philosophy at Michigan State. Greg had studied biology at Cornell University, where, after exposure to a variety of philosophies and religions, he underwent a startling conversion from secularism to Christianity. Toward the end of his Cornell years, Greg was attending an evangelical church, but began questioning the need for so many different Christian confessions. Returning to Michigan where he grew up, he started his masters program and simultaneously visited and studied several denominations. Though raised in his early years as a Roman Catholic, impressed with the church's many virtues, and drawn toward Catholic charismatic spirituality, Greg was not at peace with several Roman teachings.

I met Greg while he was resting in the microbiology lounge. My laboratory was across the hall, and the lab of Greg's father, a professor, was just a few doors down. (It also turned out that my doctoral advisor lived next door to Greg's parents!) After we had introduced ourselves and struck up a polite conversation, Greg invited me to a philosophy of science discussion group that he was organizing for a few graduate students. The group had originally been intended as a discussion group for internationals at a local church. When all but one couple backed out, however, Greg invited several other students (mostly mainland Chinese) to discuss scientific reasoning and how science interacts with larger philosophical and world-view issues. Much to his surprise, I actually showed up at the first meeting and continued coming. Our talks were lively, and we grew into a close-knit group of friends who later would go camping and gather for dinners together.

Group members often turned the discussions toward religion and theology, which helped dig up big questions that I had buried deep under my academic activities. I began wondering whether spiritual as well as scientific knowledge might be possible to attain. Some of my unquestioned assumptions about life, including my self-sufficiency and control over the future, were being brought out to face the light of day.

During the period of our discussion group, Greg providentially encountered two members of a local Orthodox mission, St. James, at an information table in the campus International Center. Intrigued, he read the available literature and visited St. James the very next Sunday. Enthused about the worship and solid doctrine he saw, Greg soon invited everyone in the discussion group to come visit the church with him. One of the wives in the group and I were the first to accept, and I attended my first Orthodox Liturgy in March of 1991. I still did not think I would become a Christian.

My early impressions of Orthodoxy included its external similarity to Buddhism (as in the use of incense and icons), the beauty of its worship, and the strong faith shown by the people of St. James. As I am not a morning person, arising early on Sunday for a long liturgical service was a challenge for me. Yet the priest's teaching was captivating, and I found myself wanting to return regularly to hear what the next homily would hold.

I was perhaps most intrigued by the teaching about Christ's suffering—that He had a most unpleasant death without having done anything wrong. That He voluntarily suffered for the specific sins of all human beings began to have meaning for me. As I've mentioned, having led a relatively comfortable life, and having seen many people become Christians during periods of personal suffering, I did not want to know God this way. However, I began to realize that knowing myself means realizing that my selfishness causes sin and suffering even in a relatively peaceful, easy life. The concept of redemption through suffering began to make sense to me.

Several months before we began dating, Greg had an unusual spiritual encounter in which he was informed that I would become his wife. Saying nothing of this to me, he sought advice from the priest at St. James, who counseled him to proceed cautiously on the revelation. We began to meet regularly to study the Scriptures and a catechism together. Our approach to the choice of a religion (for me) and a church (for Greg) was similar to scientific reasoning, where competing hypotheses are judged in the light of available evidence. I asked many questions and gradually gained in understanding of the Christian Faith.

One Gospel story that helped me was that of the Samaritan woman who begged for Christ's mercy and was told (with a smile?) that He had come for the children of Israel, to which she responded that even dogs get crumbs from the children's table. I told Greg that I was the dog, and it really dawned on me that Christ's teaching and suffering were not only for the people of His time and place, but for people of all ages.

Within nine months of first visiting St. James, Greg had been chrismated into Orthodoxy and started courting me. Though he was instrumental in my path to faith, I did not want to become Christian just for his sake, but for God's sake, because God wants our hearts set on Him.

Yes, faith was forming within me during my first year of attending church, but my decision to join the Orthodox Church took three years. During that time I visited evangelical, Episcopal, and Roman Catholic churches and talked with people about the differences between the various Christian traditions. I took only necessary interest in doctrinal disputes, and concluded that I could trust the historical authenticity of Orthodox teaching. The structured and disciplined nature of Orthodox spiritual life, as well as ancient ceremonial rites and church protocols, were difficult at first to see as liberating, but participation in them has changed this. Within the structure and discipline, I saw God's life touching ordinary people. Though some people have come and gone at St. James, a dedicated core of families has shown me the attitudes needed for overcoming the difficulties of living out faith, hope, and love.

Especially powerful to me was simply watching people go forward to receive the Eucharist. I would sit near the front and stare as others received from the cup. I always imagined what it would be like to receive the Body and Blood of Christ as they did at the Last Supper, to remember His salvation. After I realized that Greg would become my husband, I increasingly desired to experience Holy Communion with him. The children of St. James, with their angelic faces and deep trust in their parents, were also a profound influence on my desire to join the Church. They are living icons.

On Holy Saturday of 1994, I spat on Satan, and the strong arms of Father Richard Peters baptized me into the Body of Christ. Upon emerging from the waters, I was wrapped in a white robe, a shining robe of light, while purifying tears of joy poured freely down my cheeks and the cantor sang hauntingly beautiful strains. The next morning at the Feast of the Resurrection, fragrant oil was firmly crossed on my body, prayers were spoken over me, and I was free at last to go forward and receive the Eucharist. Again my tears streamed.

Having been baptized for almost two years now, I still feel like a baby learning to pray. Christian life has helped me to stabilize my view of the world, order my priorities, and become more understanding of others. Though Christianity is not for our mere comfort—indeed, we are called to hardships—I nonetheless find participation in Orthodoxy to be deeply comforting. I suppose it comes from simply knowing, and feeling, that God is with us in life's details and has provided the Church, her people and structure, as our home on earth for safe guidance to the everlasting Home.

In the summer of 1994, Gregory and I were betrothed in a brief church ceremony. He had secured my parents' blessing by visiting them for three weeks to get to know them and ask for my hand in marriage. My parents were surprisingly supportive of both my conversion and my engagement to an American—things to which many Asian parents are strongly opposed. Though they encouraged my conversion more as a means to marital unity (very important to Asians) than as a search for spiritual truth, I am glad for their blessing.

We were united by God through Father Peters at St. James in May of 1995. An unusual assortment of people, including scientists and friends from two universities, parishioners, my family from Taipei, and Greg's relatives and family friends, gathered to watch us circle the Gospel in the dance of Isaiah. My memories from the wedding are so beautiful that I fear to watch the videotape lest anything seem less than perfect. Marriage by a priest of faith in the glorious Orthodox wedding rites allowed us to feel the seal of the Holy Spirit on our union. (Also, the multiple fertility prayers appear to have been quite effective!)

And so, seven years after arriving in America as a rather self-centered and secular scientist, I find myself a Christian, a wife, an expectant mother, and still a scientist. I am very happy. I look forward in hope to a lifetime of enjoying the companionship of marriage, raising children, sharing with wonderful Christian friends, studying science, and encouraging others to discover the treasures of Orthodox Christianity. It is good to find Home. Thanks be to God.

Yuen-tsu Yu Velicer lives with her husband Gregory in Lansing, Michigan. Their first child is expected to arrive in July of 1996. The Velicers attend St. James Orthodox Church in Williamston, Michigan. Yuen-tsu enjoys reading, hiking and camping, swimming, and volleyball. She remains close to her parents in Taipei, her younger brother at the University of Pennsylvania, and her parish family at St. James.

∞ Elizabeth*

Blessed Be the Name of the Lord

It was a typical bedroom of the sixties, painted in neon yellow and green, plastered with torn-out teen-magazine pictures of models in hip-huggers with flower-painted faces, the Monkees, and other pop icons. The "mod" look was in, and so were "Jesus freaks." I didn't consider myself a Jesus freak, but by the standards of the day, as a sixteen-year-old who loved the Lord, I might be mistaken for a freak. On this particular day, the breeze gently whipped the cotton curtains through my open window as I sat reading the Bible.

Feeling completely enveloped by the love of God, I closed my Bible and instinctively kissed the cover. "Hmmm, that was a strange thing to do," I thought to myself. If Jesus had been physically present I would have hugged Him, but since I couldn't hug Him, kissing His words, His truth, seemed right. I didn't know then that this had actually been the standard practice of Christians since the earliest days of the Church.

My spiritual journey had begun much earlier. Mother

surname withheld

45

single-handedly parented us while Dad served in the Army, and it was she who shared Bible stories and prayed with my brother and me at bedtime, as her parents had done with her. Although Mom grew up in a family that occasionally attended church, our family did not. After Dad returned from the Army, we moved, so my brother and I walked alone to the neighborhood church for Sunday School.

My life began to change when, as a high-school student, I was invited to a church retreat with a girl-friend in another city. There for the first time I heard that God had a plan for my life, and that I could respond to Him personally by inviting Christ into my heart. This I did, genuinely excited to learn of a Savior who cared for me. As is so common, however, I soon came down from that mountain-top experience into the valley of reality. At the retreat I had learned about the God of the Bible, and He seemed very real; I longed to know Him better. But I was on my own, not knowing what to do next.

By the time I was sixteen, I had attended many different churches, and I was very confused. For a while I stopped going to church altogether. During this time of uncertainty, I began to date a young man; he was outspoken in his Christian beliefs, and insisted we attend church together. I admired his forthright ways. When he left for college I continued to attend his church and grow in my Christian life, thanks to the dynamic youth pastor and the teens in the youth group.

Most of my senior year of high school I was starry-eyed, as I enjoyed being courted by this college-aged boy with great manners and top grades. We thought we were in love, but looking back I realize our attachment to each other was made strong because we were both looking for a way to escape unhappy home situations. In any event, marriage seemed like the perfect way to get away from home.

It didn't take long into our marriage to realize that all of our problems hadn't dried up and disappeared. Indeed, the problems went deeper than either one of us knew; all we'd done was to trade old struggles for new ones. In the beginning, infatuation blinded me to the warning signs of infidelity. But during our first year of marriage, my husband had an affair with a classmate from the Christian college he attended. After seeking counseling, I began making arrangements to return home. But he promised to end the affair, and said we'd start over again at a new location far from where we had been living. We moved, but our problems moved with us.

Eventually, finding myself living within a difficult marriage, I became active in church. I tried to be present whenever the doors were open. As the years rolled by, immersion in church life became an escape. Witnessing for Christ, Bible studies, teaching children's classes, memorizing Scripture verses and in general trying to be a good Christian wife afforded me a measure of control and comfort. My suffering did bring me closer to God, as well, and I trusted in His love and care. It occurred to me, of course, to end the marriage, but after seven years we had two children and I couldn't bear the thought of taking them away from their father. In the circles I ran in, the unspoken assumption was that "Christians do not divorce." With counsel and stiff determination I decided to stick it out.

My husband had long since quit attending church. He was very charming and persuasive, so it took a long time for me to become suspicious of other adulterous affairs, and even longer for those suspicions to be confirmed. It was fourteen years before I realized he had serious drug problems. Finding hypodermic needles forced me to face his drug addiction. His actions eventually became exaggerated, and in his paranoia he would stalk me. Even more frightening, he told me he had been receiving death threats against everyone in the family because of unpaid gambling debts. It was surreal. I wondered, "How could this be happening to me?"

We sought marriage counseling in order to bring about change, but after yet another year, even the Christian counselor offered us no hope. During that last-ditch effort the problems continued to escalate. So, after fifteen years of battles and deception, I called a lawyer to prepare for divorce. My marriage was over. My ideals were crushed, and exhaustion replaced determination.

Divorce is painful no matter what the circumstances are, but I had no idea just how serious the consequences of this decision would be. What I envisioned was that we would split up and go our own ways, sharing child custody and working out other snags and adjustments. Though I gave assent to the truth that God is "good but not safe," as C.S. Lewis expressed it, I still believed that if I lived as a faithful Christian nothing truly bad would happen to me, and this nightmare would pass.

On a cold and rainy autumn morning, all my ideas about what to expect from God, and what it meant to be a Christian, were forever changed. As I was on my way to work, my ex-husband, in disguise, leapt out at me, stabbed me repeatedly, left me for dead, and fled. A good Samaritan stopped to help, moving me to his car and then rushing me to a nearby hospital. My parents were contacted and the children taken to a safe location, as he wanted to abduct them. For hours, I underwent surgery on my chest, breast, arms, and hands. When my parents asked about my condition, they were told there was doubt I would survive.

Regaining consciousness after surgery, I felt as if I were coming out of a long dark tunnel. Although I awoke to intense pain, I was also overwhelmed with a profound sense of the presence and faithfulness of God. There was no question in my mind that it was He who had saved me.

Over the next couple of months the injuries healed, the divorce was finalized, and my ex-husband was sent to prison. On the surface, upon returning home and going back to work and church, I began to put my life and faith back in order. Although outwardly I went through the motions, the gross shock of the attack made dull and remote almost everything that I had come to believe about God and Christianity.

As time passed, with its comforting routine of daily responsibilities, I grew stronger physically and emotionally. One day a friend approached me and asked if she could give my phone number to an old acquaintance. From my very first telephone conversation with this man, we felt the hand of God on us. Becoming good friends, then falling in love, followed quite naturally. When he proposed marriage I rejoiced, even though it looked as though we would have to wait until he fulfilled an academic commitment in Europe. Absence knit our hearts even closer once he moved to Europe, however, so our plans changed. We were keeping the phone company and postal service in business!

I flew to join him several months sooner than originally planned, and we married in a beautiful ceremony surrounded by my husband's new friends. They even threw a surprise reception for us, complete with a wedding cake, music, and gifts of love and support.

After our lengthy honeymoon the children flew to Europe, and together we built a new life in a beautiful and historic European city. Our first home was on the edge of a woodland. I remember hearing the shouts of the children's laughter in mid-winter, as they tobogganed down the knolls in their brightly colored jackets.

Far from the scene of the crime in this new location,

I attempted to take hold of my new beginning. The experience of new love and all the time in the world to go to the ballet, the opera, art galleries, and museums suspended the horror of the recent past. Life had never been better. I had long given up the dream of traveling to Europe, but here I was, sometimes feeling as if I were living in a romance novel.

However, the pain of the attack had never completely dissipated. In the safe environment of being loved, grief, fear, and rage mounted. Flashbacks replayed daily. Eventually, panic attacks sent me into collapse. The fear was so gripping that I walked with my eyes downcast, afraid to look into the eyes of people around me. "Is there someone else who wants to leap out and murder me?" I'd think. Thoughts of suicide were constant companions, tempting me to flee from the painful aftershocks and suffering.

In the midst of this, God seemed silent. Faith had always been something I thought was within my own control, but I began to realize it was beyond my power even to believe. I prayed that God wouldn't let me fall away. Exhausted, I felt myself on the edge of insanity. I had come to a point eloquently described by Metropolitan Anthony Bloom:

> God is there at the point of greatest tension, at
> the breaking point, at the center of the storm.
> In a way despair is at the center of things—if

only we are prepared to go through it. . . . The
day when God is absent, when He is silent—
that is the beginning of prayer. Not when we
have a lot to say, but when we say to God "I
can't live without You, why are You so cruel,
so silent?" This knowledge that we must find
or die—that makes us break through to the
place where we are in the Presence.

Compelled by this crisis, my husband and I con-
fided in a young Christian Czechoslovakian couple
who lived down the hall from us in our apartment
complex. The four of us decided to pray together daily,
expecting that through prayer I would be strengthened
and find relief.

Joseph and Michaela were Orthodox catechumens.
The first evening we arrived at their door, the aroma of
incense drifted out to greet us. Joseph said they had
already begun to pray for us in preparation for our time
together. They had lit candles, giving a warm, peaceful
glow to their small apartment. In the corner of their
living room, which doubled as a bedroom, were two
small icons.

We sat down and they began to talk about the
importance of praying often. Several prayers would be
of help, they told me, and I would learn those in time.
But for now, one particular prayer would be most
powerful. I was to pray it as much as possible, especially when I became troubled, preceding it by making
the sign of the cross over myself so as to mark myself as

a child of God. They then presented me with a prayer rope and showed me how to pray, "Lord Jesus Christ, Son of God, have mercy on me a sinner" each time I came to a knot. The rope would anchor my attention and keep my mind from wandering.

While facing the icons, the four of us knelt and prayed. After leaving the apartment that first night, I felt that a piece of armor had been given to me to aid in spiritual battle. From that point on we met every night for a week. At the end of each prayer time, they presented me with a small gift to keep me remembering God's truths.

I found much comfort in outward acts, such as lighting a candle when offering a prayer, especially when Joseph explained that it is a symbol that we are reflecting the Light of Christ. "You are the light of the world . . . let your light so shine before men, that they may see your good works and glorify your Father in heaven" (Matthew 5:14-16). Candles also served as a visual reminder that God was watching over me and hearing my prayers; when I saw the flickering flame I felt reassured that God hadn't forgotten me. In that flame was His promise, "I will never leave you nor forsake you" (Hebrews 13:5).

Joseph and Michaela gave me one particular gift I highly value, an icon of Christ being taken down from the Cross. At first I was confused by the icon. It depicted a depressing moment—the disciples facing the utter hopelessness of a dead Savior. Seemingly absent from this icon was the hope of salvation.

But Joseph explained, "Right now, you have no hope. You do not know in three days there will be resurrection, hope, and life. Your reality is in this icon. I promise you, your days of grief and despair will come to an end. So when you pray in front of this icon, remember that although Mary and the others attending Christ couldn't see the outcome of the Crucifixion, you can."

A surge of faith swept through me as I trusted for a peace not yet realized. At first, as I prayed in front of the icon, I didn't "feel" the power of the Resurrection, but I believed its joy would come. To this day, that icon gives me hope and courage to face the uncertainty of the future.

About this time, we asked Joseph and Michaela if we could meet their priest-monk, Father Theodoros, hoping perhaps he could help us with the aftermath of the attack and teach us more about Orthodoxy. Our first meeting took place in his humble studio apartment. Father Theodoros had long white hair (typical for a monk) and sky-blue eyes. He greeted us warmly. Pouring us a small amount of brandy, he toasted the warmth of friendship. An experienced and wise man, he knew that the brandy would help to calm me.

To be honest, I felt so undone I half expected an exorcism on the spot! But instead, gentle Father Theodoros listened, asked questions, and prayed, spending most of the afternoon with us. He invited us to see his parish chapel, located in the basement of the apartment house. There he prayed for me, anointing my forehead, mouth, eyes, ears, and hands with oil. After a blessing, he led us to the front door with an invitation to call him anytime.

Peace and quiet authority surrounded this monk; we longed for more, so we began to meet with him regularly. Guiding me through a labyrinth of emotions and thoughts, he would point out specific ways God was lavishing His lovingkindness on us in the midst of suffering. "Your husband is a gift and a resource from God; thank Him," he would remind me. Thereafter, every time I looked upon my husband I would thank God for him, and my focus began to change. Father Theodoros seemed to know I could digest only a little at a time, and he walked with me step by step. He stood in the long-existent tradition of gracious, godly Orthodox guidance that is both discerning and humble.

One important point Father Theodoros emphasized repeatedly: Healing would come from inside the Church; that is where the Holy Spirit dwells. The Fathers tell us that the Church is like a hospital where we go to be healed. He went on to explain that suffering is just part of life and shouldn't surprise us. In the "communion of saints," we find so many who have suffered before us, having run the race, fought the good fight, and finished triumphantly. We are not alone in our struggles, for this whole heavenly host is interceding for us.

Our family began to worship at the Orthodox church.

I remember our first Sunday, hearing the chanting as we entered. Our children looked at us with surprise and wonder; the incense blanketed the room with its sweet aroma. My husband explained to the children how incense is a picture of our prayers ascending to heaven ("Let my prayer be set before you as incense"— Psalm 141:2). The children were captivated as they studied the icons, watched the burning candles, and observed the movements of the priest at the altar. Their senses were fully engaged, and they liked this kind of worship.

In the meantime, I was noticing something quite different about the service. Whenever I heard Christ mentioned, it was in union with the Father and the Holy Spirit. At first I was uncomfortable with the fact that the prayers didn't end with "in Jesus' Name, Amen." Christ had been the cornerstone in my former churches, the only way to salvation. Was Christ behind it all in this church, too? I began to look around me, and saw the answer was literally staring me in the face.

Christ was in front of the church on each side of the altar. On the left, He was sitting in the arms of Mary as she gestured toward Him, guiding us to God Incarnate, her Savior and ours. On the right, He looked directly at us, beckoning us with the Gospel open to John 14:6 ("I am the way, the truth, and the life. No one comes to the Father except through Me"). The icons of the church were clearly theology in image form. In Orthodoxy, theology is how our faith is lived out practically. It is in the prayers and music, in the whole of our lives.

In truth, it seemed Christ permeated the Divine Liturgy. Every prayer ended, "In the Name of the Father, and of the Son, and of the Holy Spirit." Clearly, Christ *was* receiving all glory, power, and honor due Him, and so were the other members of the Trinity, as the "consubstantial, co-eternal, and undivided" whole.

Four months after our first Orthodox Liturgy, my husband fulfilled his professional obligation and we left Europe. Difficult as it was for all of us to go, we returned to the States refreshed and ready to begin again. My husband started a new job, we enrolled the children in school, and we hunted for an Orthodox parish. Thanks be to God, after only a month or so in our new church, our entire family decided to be chrismated—on Orthodoxy Sunday, no less!

Then the following year, again on Orthodoxy Sunday, we brought our newborn daughter for Holy Baptism. I have been so blessed to witness her budding love and faith in her Creator and Redeemer as it is wondrously formed in the sacramental life and community of the Church. We all continue to strive to submit to the yoke of this path of salvation. Though it is arduous, it is joyful and breathes in us renewed health and life, both spiritual and physical.

Our entrance into Holy Orthodoxy has had various effects on our old Protestant friends and family members. It seems, in general, that those who are not Christian, including many family members, are indifferent or curious. But for a number of our Protestant friends, Orthodoxy seems like just a more exotic version of Roman Catholicism, and is therefore viewed with great suspicion. Out of politeness these friends may ask about "church," but in general they avoid any religious discussions. I am finding it increasingly difficult to cultivate intimate relationships with friends who, out of fear or perhaps ignorance, are unwilling to explore what I've learned about the historic, Apostolic Church. Because it has changed me and has become such an important part of me, if I am not free to express myself, my friends don't truly know me.

And now? Now I realize that profound suffering helped me to see what was lacking in myself and in my Protestant tradition, opening my eyes to the truth and beauty of Orthodoxy. Suffering broke down my illusions and humbled me. I learned that I needed healing—not just from the attack, but from deep needs within myself.

It took the attack to get me to the right "hospital," and now that I'm there, I'm not left in a bare room to fend for myself. Weekly, I can avail myself of the Eucharist, true medicine for the soul; confession, the cleansing of conscience; icons, mediators of grace and encouragement; the saints, prayer warriors and examples. Filled with the Holy Spirit, who works within the Traditions of the Church, I have been caught up in the mystery and the beauty of Orthodox Christianity.

Although the healing of soul and body continues, I will again be tempted to fear my ex-husband's sworn statement of revenge, as his release date from prison moves closer. It is a continual challenge to be at peace and to trust God for the future. But I think that's exactly where God wants each of us to be, on the living edge, trusting Him for all things. Blessed be the Name of the Lord!

For obvious reasons, Elizabeth must keep most information about herself veiled. However, she has been enjoying living "happily ever after" (which does include dirty dishes) for the past five years in a village where she is involved in women's ministries and iconography. She is currently at work completing the iconostasis for her church.

∞ Susan Engelhardt

From Rome to Home

I was in college during Vatican II. It was an exciting time, because it had been nearly a century since the last council of the Roman Catholic Church, and we were all avidly following the proceedings. A priest at my university (St. Michael's College in the University of Toronto) provided weekly updates on what was transpiring.

Very few people realized at the time how far Vatican II would undermine what piety the Roman church had retained in the centuries since the Great Schism of 1054. The initial changes seemed slight. There was experimentation with guitar music at Mass, and discussions of whether one had to go to Mass on Sunday to fulfill one's Sunday obligation (the duty imposed on every Catholic of attending Mass on Sundays). One friend said any day during the week was acceptable, as long as one attended Mass weekly. But much that was traditional in the church still remained. I married in 1965 with a full seminary choir singing everything in Latin.

Then came further changes. I liked the idea of an English Mass, but found the liturgical music in Latin exceptionally beautiful; there was nothing comparable in English. In addition, the English translation for the new Mass was banal. It failed to convey an attitude of reverence before the holiness of God. There was little sense of piety. Then, in 1970, the Tridentine (Latin) Mass (created in 1570 in an attempt to abolish innovations and restore the Mass to its more ancient forms) was effectively prohibited. The remnants of the fasts, which dated from the time of the Apostles and the Fathers, were also set aside.

In the late 1970s and early 1980s, when I began to teach in Sunday school, I was told that not just the disciplines of the church, but many traditional beliefs could be revised. The Roman Catholic understanding of the development of doctrine meant that new teachings could be discovered by theologians. In effect, the Roman church could create a church with commitments different from those of the Fathers.

By this time the church in which I had grown up had changed radically. Many of the priests I had known while growing up had left the priesthood, married, and become deeply disillusioned. When I was a girl, high schools were full of boys and girls looking forward to becoming priests and nuns. There were 10.73 seminarians per 10,000 Roman Catholics in 1965, as compared to only 0.84 per 10,000 in 1995.

The Roman church was deviating ever farther from the piety of my youth. Sermons on Sundays began to focus more on political and social issues than on spiritual matters. Church became more of a political seminar than a guide to holiness. When discussions did focus on matters spiritual, they often undermined the traditions of Christianity.

Many people became interested in ordaining Christian priestesses and blessing homosexual unions. There was a deep anger at the divinely established equality-in-hierarchy in the relationship between men and women. (I later learned that Orthodoxy gives no basis for liberation theology or for feminism in the family or in Church affairs. Though it is very clear that men and women are acknowledged as equal—indeed, no human being is honored more than the Theotokos—there is a hierarchy of authority and order between men and women, as set forth in numerous passages of Scripture.)

Some also worked to undermine the divinely established significance of sexuality, dismissing the idea that any kind of sexual union could be considered perverted. I knew something was wrong in the church, but did not know what the remedy was. How could I reconcile this lack of spirituality with my belief in the Roman church as the true apostolic church?

It was during a sabbatical year spent in Berlin in 1988-89 that my husband, Tristram, came into contact with Orthodoxy. That year, we decided to spend Christmas in Constantinople (Istanbul) and chose to attend Liturgy with the Orthodox Ecumenical Patriarch on

Christmas Day. My husband was beginning to recognize that the Roman church could not possibly be the Church of the Apostles and Fathers, partly because of the experiences he'd had with Catholic bishops and theologians during his tenure as medical ethics advisor on a committee for the International Federation of Catholic Universities.

So we found ourselves in a taxi in Constantinople, traveling to the humble quarters of the Phanar, the residence of the Patriarch. The tourists were numerous, the believers few, and everything very strange. The darkness, the incense, and all the hair on the clergy made it seem so foreign to me. There were a few points of similarity with the Mass, but it was far more strange than familiar.

When we were back home again, my husband said that we would start attending Orthodox Liturgy instead of Mass. I agreed because I knew that, although I would not be able to receive Communion in the Orthodox Church, I could at least fulfill my Sunday obligation by attending there. The Liturgy remained strange to me, but I followed my husband and tried to accustom myself to it while waiting for this fad to end. But it never did!

A year later, my husband announced that he and two of our three daughters were converting to Orthodoxy. My reaction was negative, to say the least. How could he desert the church of our youth, the true apostolic church, which (as I had been taught) the Orthodox had left in 1054?

Tristram kept explaining to me that it was the Romans who had left the Orthodox, and that the history taught to me all through parochial school had been incorrect. I thoroughly objected to this new version of history. Besides, I had a great deal of difficulty being patient with the length of the Orthodox services. Soon my husband insisted on attending Saturday evening Great Vespers also. Going to church *twice?* If there had been a way to rebel, I would have. A few times I tried going to Mass while he went to Liturgy, but I found being by myself unsatisfactory.

So he converted (taking the Orthodox name of Herman), along with two daughters. I attended and watched, thinking all along that this was a terrible mistake. We continued going to church for both Vespers and Liturgy. My one consolation during this period was that I enjoy singing and at least I could sing during the services. The music was lovely and very different from anything I had ever heard or learned. It was only several years later that I discovered that church music joins with the angels who are eternally praising God. That is why there is nothing comparable to it in secular music.

My husband was very persistent. He kept pointing out a fact here and a fact there, all reasons why Orthodoxy is the True Faith. Universal papal jurisdiction is a Roman innovation. The Roman doctrine of the *filioque* (the eternal procession of the Spirit from the Father *and the Son*) is a heresy. Papal infallibility is a Roman innovation. The doctrine of the immaculate conception of

Mary is based on a misunderstanding of the nature of original sin. And for each of these points and more, he would go into very clear, reasonable detail about the history of each doctrine, continually underscoring how the Western Church had separated itself from the spirituality of the early Church and the Fathers. My reaction was to think that he was preaching heresy.

Yet I had to admit, he was making sense. As we debated, I learned that the doctrine of universal papal jurisdiction was unknown in the early Church. As St. Cyprian of Carthage (d. 257) stressed in his treatise, "The Unity of the Church," "Surely the rest of the Apostles also were that which Peter was, endowed with an equal partnership of office and of power."

No one in the early Church would have entertained the notion of papal infallibility. One pope, Honorius, was condemned for heresy by the Sixth Ecumenical Council in A.D. 692, so he obviously was not infallible.

The doctrine of the *filioque,* the view that the Holy Spirit proceeds eternally from the Father *and* the Son, was also a novelty. The Orthodox Church continues to teach the Creed formulated by the Council of Constantinople (A.D. 381), which expresses the clear force of the Gospel of St. John: "the Spirit of truth who proceeds from the Father" (John 15:26).

The belief in Mary's immaculate conception turns on a mistranslation of Paul's Epistle to the Romans (5:12), which suggests in the Latin that not only the consequences, but the *guilt* of Adam's sin were passed on to all future generations. As a result, the Catholics found it necessary to insulate Mary from that guilt so that she could be a fit receptacle for God, born without the stain of Adam and Eve's sin. The Orthodox, on the other hand, recognize that though we are all burdened with a sinful and broken nature because of Adam and Eve, we do not participate in their guilt. We are guilty of our own sins.

I began to understand that the Roman Catholic Church wasn't truly Catholic in the historically understood sense of the word ("what has been believed by all Christians in all places, at all times"). They had built one novel doctrine upon another until they had created a new religion.

Ironically, the key that opened my mind to Orthodoxy turned out to be reason, the very foundation of the Roman church. In the Roman tradition, one reasons to every conclusion. And I had been raised and taught to use my reason to come to logical conclusions, one of which was that the Roman Catholic Church was the true church. Now, little by little, my husband chipped away at the logic of what I'd been taught. Frequently, I became impatient and told him not ever to say another word about religion! He never listened, but only waited until I had calmed down, which took perhaps a week, then started in on me again. Everyone knows that water wears away stone. I was that stone, and the water was incessant, gentle, and oh, so reasonable.

Two years after he became Orthodox, I finally decided my husband was right and that Orthodoxy was indeed the True Faith. I arranged with our parish priest to be chrismated just before Easter, as a surprise for my husband. One evening, we simply stayed late after Vespers and I entered the One True Church. That was my intellectual conversion. But now that I had opened the door and been sealed by the Spirit, I began my spiritual conversion, my change of mind, my repentance, my *metanoia*. This second dimension was completely different. I had no idea what would happen in the months to come or what a difference Orthodoxy would make in my attitudes. But, as St. John Climacus says in *The Ladder of Divine Ascent*, I had found the bottom of the ladder and was ready to start climbing.

My husband had started going to Matins, and after I converted, he wanted me to accompany him. I groaned and moaned and refused, so we continued going to church in two cars. Whenever I tried to get up earlier on Sunday, I would have a strong negative reaction and even become angry. Then I began having a recurrent dream: I was walking up an incline, bent nearly double because I was pulling a fishnet that held a howling, thrashing person endeavoring in every way possible to stop my progress. I thought of it as my Orthodox self forcing my Roman Catholic self to become truly Orthodox. It took about six months before the dream ceased.

It was a long time before I could realize and appreciate how different Roman Catholicism, and Western Christianity in general, had become from the Church of the Fathers. Changes began as early as A.D. 867, when St. Photius the Great of Constantinople excommunicated Pope Nicholas I of Rome for changing the apostolic fasts, not allowing married men to be priests, separating confirmation from baptism, and accepting the heretical understanding of the *filioque*.

The West had already begun its journey away from the lived mystical experience of union with God to a legalistic approach to sin and a scholastic understanding of theology. In Roman Catholicism, mysticism is not central. It does not supply the core of the Tradition, nor is union with God (theosis) clearly appreciated as the focus of the Christian life. In fact, Roman Catholic theology had become not something that was lived, but the scholarly undertaking of academicians. Many of those theologians were bent on academic discoveries that could make the Church of the Fathers conform to contemporary life.

By the time I had been Orthodox for a year, I started to realize that my spiritual conversion was underway. While Roman Catholic, I said one decade of the rosary every day. When I became Orthodox, I asked the priest to bless my continuing to say the rosary—which he did, explaining that I must use the Orthodox version of the prayers (the Lord's Prayer, Hail Mary, and Glory Be). By the time a year was up, I realized that the Orthodox prayer life was very different from, and so much richer than, the Roman Catholic prayers. The rosary was simply not an appropriate way to pray, and I stopped.

My father also passed away from cancer in those first years after my conversion. It was heart-wrenching for me to watch, because I had been Orthodox long enough to recognize the inadequacy of the Roman Catholic approach to preparation for death. My father's pastor, a man truly striving to be pious, would visit my father in the hospital and talk to him a bit about secular matters, say a short prayer, and give him Communion. There was no real repentance on my father's part, no attempt to free the heart from passions so as to be united with God. This weighed on me heavily. I prayed for him with all my heart and strength, since he had no one else who was praying with or for him as he died. Before I became Orthodox, I never could have understood the need for continual, sincere repentance from sin, for turning to God with full love. I never could have understood the need always to prepare for death, because we never know when the Bridegroom is coming.

By this time, it had finally become a joy to attend Vespers and Matins. It was no longer difficult to get out of bed; the hours in church passed so quickly, I could hardly comprehend where the time had gone. I increased my reading about Orthodoxy, realizing that my youngest daughter, who still lived at home, was far more Orthodox in her outlook than I was, and that I had not yet put my mind in my heart.

Around this time, I began reading Eusebius' *History of the Church* with a friend. When my friend did not understand something, my daughter could explain the

Orthodox position clearly, while I merely sat there in wonder that I was still so far from my daughter's kind of comprehension.

In Orthodoxy, I learned that knowing God comes with prayer, fasting, and participation in the Holy Mysteries, more than through intellectual effort. Theological knowledge is found in the love of God. I lead my life now just trying to learn humility, the most difficult and essential of the virtues, as I work at totally submitting to God.

Susan Engelhardt holds a B.A. in philosophy from the University of Toronto and an M.A. in German from the University of Texas. She is one of the co-organizers of the Deutsche Samstagsschule (a Saturday school teaching German to children) in Houston, and has been a Girl Scout volunteer since 1976. She teaches Sunday School and is a member of her parish choir.

CD Jeanne Harper

The Pearl of Great Price

One of the biggest surprises of my life is to be
granted a major discovery late in life. It still amazes me!
My husband and I have had this privilege, and what
follows is our story. Let me tell you why discovering
Orthodoxy has brought me such joy.

I heard the evangelical gospel as a music student in
London, and with all my heart truly accepted that the
Bible is the Word of God, not to be tampered with and
utterly reliable. I am grateful that I was schooled in the
two W's—Word and Witness. Yet all along I confess I
yearned for a third W, worship, which unfortunately
did not figure too prominently in evangelical circles. I
desperately wanted a more contemplative, adoring faith,
and I warmed to books like Brother Lawrence's *Practicing the Presence of God*.

Some years later, in 1962, my husband Michael and
I became involved in the charismatic renewal movement in the Anglican Church. My spiritual longing was
satisfied in great measure as we found ourselves relating far more tangibly and specifically to the Holy Spirit,

as well as to God the Father. Many aspects of our lives were revitalized by this new appreciation for the work of the Spirit. In the meetings of the Fountain Trust, an interchurch organization my husband had founded with the blessing of the Anglican bishop of London, we witnessed miracles, as well as healings, visions, and deliverances. My prayer life was revitalized, I grew a great deal in my knowledge of the Holy Spirit's guidance, and I led a prayer network called the Lydia Fellowship for a number of years.

As the charismatic renewal spread, we could see that it was at least addressing the dry intellectualism that so often characterizes the churches of the West. There was no denying that the gifts of the Holy Spirit in those days were authentic and had a powerful effect in people's lives, all without forfeiting scriptural truth. In those early years of the Fountain Trust, we felt like children on uncharted seas, very dependent on God, who was constantly surprising us and doing the unpredictable.

Our fellowship was a joy that did not lessen even as this work of God spread through the country. But I can see now that, even though we had more of the third W, there was another huge problem that had hardly been touched—that of true Church authority and unity. Michael had noticed it from the beginning. He had seen the Church as the true Body of Christ, as he studied what for him became a life-changing passage of Scripture: Ephesians 3:14-21. "The Church is not *like* the Body of Christ, it *is* the Body of Christ," he began to say.

Out of this he developed a concern for Christian unity, and his second book, *Power for the Body of Christ*, highlighted this.

Yet individualism was in our bones, quite unrecognized for what it is: inimical to the Kingdom of God. The idea of an unbroken, undivided Body of Christ was academic. We were, after all, rejoicing in our new relationship with God, understanding the Word with a fresh clarity, and enjoying our free, easily singable worship songs. We even had new freedom in our Anglican liturgical services, room being made in their structure for spontaneous prayer, praise, and gifts of the Spirit.

But with all that, there was still the problem of the wider church scene. I remember longing for more discipline, for a voice of true authority when issues of national importance arose. It seemed our leaders could do or undo anything, and then carry on as though all were well. Our roots were only as deep as the latest clerical whim. So we did our own thing, and the charismatic renewal did not have the impact we had expected.

While we still lived in hope that whatever had been wrong could be corrected, a bombshell dropped which had irreversible consequences. I was at a small meeting which was interrupted in order that we could see on TV the result of the voting of the General Synod of the Church of England on the issue of the ordination of women. At that time, I had not thought very much of the controversy, nor had I worked out its implications.

But during the hush after the vote, which approved women's ordination, I quietly ceased to be an Anglican in my heart. This seemed an act of rebellion on the deepest level, that of creation. Not one of the dozen or so of us watching the television looked at the others or showed any reaction.

It was some time before Michael and I could even bring ourselves to compare notes. But when we finally did, out of our sharing and a sabbatical that followed in early 1993 came the book, *Equal and Different*. It contains a theological, historical response to the Anglican Church's ordination of women. For us, this was a watershed issue. God's plan for the family and the unique makeup of men and women had been uppermost in my mind since that fateful day I heard the archbishop's announcement.

I could see that society was already being turned upside down by the refusal to recognize that men and women are inherently and comprehensively different. It seemed that treating them as identical brought great pressure on women, and even more on men, rather than adding to their contentment and happiness. Scientists and the purveyors of immorality were even offering a way around God-given, biological gender differences. I did not want to be a part of a church that went down that road.

By the time of our book's publication, I was a disaffected Anglican, but that is not what led me to the Orthodox Church. The ordination of women was the catalyst, the trigger that sent me in the direction of what deep down I had been searching for. Along with many others, I was turning from the *extempore* style of worship, prayer, and preaching that always has to be upbeat. I was looking for the traditional again.

We had had contact with Orthodox priests in Eastern Europe and the Middle East as part of preparing for an international ecumenical conference which my husband chaired in 1991. Through this contact I came to realize that the Orthodox Church has had an unbroken witness since it was founded by Christ in the first century. This realization, along with my love of history, led me to read the book, *The Orthodox Church* by Bishop Kallistos Ware. It describes this first Church through the centuries, and I felt I could see the reasons why Orthodoxy had kept the purity of the Faith.

So many of my past frustrations seemed to be resolved in the teaching and practice of the Orthodox Church. The foundation of truth was established, the authority structure was in place, basic doctrine simply was not debated; and if a priest or a bishop erred, discipline was appropriate and immediate.

Another reason for the Church's purity, I felt, was the level of persecution it had endured, and in many countries still endures. As Bishop Ware pointed out, the Orthodox Church has been a suffering Church, with four major persecutions since the East-West split in 1054: by Islam, the Crusaders, the Ottoman Empire, and communism. Sometimes the oppression was subtle, sometimes violent. Often the authorities deprived the Orthodox of their priests and destroyed their churches. Yet in those harsh circumstances, believers had an anchor that no persecutor could take away from them: their liturgy. Everyone from the simplest farmer to the most educated intellectual knew the Truth, for the daily services are packed with Scripture. They all knew the Word of God, even without a sermon, which often went unsaid due to lack of priests.

As I began to experience Orthodox worship for myself, I found the ancient set prayers both beautiful and powerfully relevant. The celebration of the Lord's Supper, or Divine Liturgy as it is called by the Orthodox, is the Church's entry into heaven in the Spirit. It is quite unmatched by anything I have experienced before, yet it is a set liturgy, unaltered for centuries.

I also came to believe Orthodoxy had kept the Faith because it is a Church that has never initiated schism. Of course, she has known separation, but only because others have left her. So I was not surprised to see in the Orthodox Church an ability to be flexible while holding to the essentials of the Faith. Orthodoxy acknowledges that truth is often paradoxical and always has an element of mystery. The Church has walked the difficult line, discerning between what cannot be changed and what is secondary. Likewise, she adheres to high standards for Christian living, but shows compassion and flexibility for the individual believer coming to confession.

I couldn't help but notice that the Orthodox Church

never experienced a Reformation. She has never denied justification by faith. In this and other respects, the Church did not need the corrective measures of the reformers. As one involved in the charismatic renewal, I was also thrilled to see that the Church had not forgotten the Holy Spirit. In Orthodox writings, modern and ancient, there is an openness to the charismatic dimension of ministry and life. The saints' lives, from the first to the twentieth century, evidence the supernatural work of God. Yet this is always divinely tempered with the typical Orthodox humility that waits for God's grace rather than actively seeking a spiritual experience.

As a child of the evangelical world, I was glad to learn in my reading of the many countries evangelized by Orthodox missionaries in the past. Yet concern for "numbers" is not Orthodox, I discovered, and I greatly appreciated an approach to evangelism that has never been frenetic. At a service there is such an awareness of the communion of saints that the number of people present is not on anyone's mind. The living presence of the saints through the ages, as represented through the icons, means that if there are only two people present, there are still millions in church that day.

I think there is, however, a growing realization among the Orthodox generally that the old missionary fervor of the past needs to be revived. Maybe Christ's words that we are not to cast our pearls before swine have been interpreted too comprehensively. A young Arabic cantor said to us one day after Vespers, "Thank you for coming" (i.e. to us in the Orthodox Church). "We have stood beside our treasure chest for so long and you are making us open it and share the treasure."

And what a treasure it is! Perhaps we should not be surprised at the continual conflicts and tensions that hinder unity and evangelism within Orthodoxy. For there are "bodiless powers" who know how priceless the treasure is and want to keep it hidden and unshared.

It is becoming more recognized that ethnicity is the main factor that has kept the treasure hidden. Because of political unrest, Orthodox believers left their homelands over the past century or so, and each ethnic group established its own church in the host countries. This did not make good soil for peace and harmony or for mission, and is not even in line with the Church's Canon Law. We pray that someday all Orthodox of each nation will be united under one episcopal government. Then the Spirit will be able to move more freely to draw others in.

As we became convinced that the Orthodox Church was our true home, we discovered that the Church—rightly—does not make it too easy for those knocking at their door to come in. Like the catechumens of old, one must demonstrate one's sincerity and commitment over a period of time. In addition, one needs patience for other possible delays. Now that I am Orthodox I understand the wariness in receiving us independent-minded, individualistic Westerners! But with the knowledge of the church scene I had accumulated over the years, there was nowhere else I wanted to go. Being kept in uncertainty as to whether or not we would be received into the Orthodox Church only strengthened my longing.

But the time for our reception came at last. Our bishop said to us recently, "The door is wide open for all to come," and he opened his arms wide. Orthodoxy is a call on all of one's life all the time. The annual cycle of feasts, fasts, and saints' days, the constant celebration, repentance, and the pilgrimages are part and parcel of Orthodox spirituality. I am not allowed to forget for very long that I am in Christ, and I am glad about that. Every important part of the Christian Faith and of the life of our Lord is highlighted in the liturgical calendar, and remembered in prayers, praises, and special services.

One of the greatest blessings I personally have found in the Orthodox Church has been the music. I am a trained musician, and music is obviously important to me. I have attended many liturgies and other services in Orthodox churches, and have often felt I was singing the songs and praying the prayers of the early Christians. The Church teaches that instrumental accompaniment, elaborate musical arrangements, or anything else that draws attention to a human being rather than to God's Word expressed in the Scriptures and hymns, all detract from the worshipper's ability to worship in spirit and in truth. I have found this to be true in my own experience. The ancient songs have stood the test of time and I applaud their use.

This approach to music reflects a characteristic that pervades all of Orthodoxy: humility. I think I love my Church because of this quality almost more than anything else. For in the context of worship, gentleness and humility are the only proper attitudes. When these qualities are present, the Lord, who said He Himself was "gentle and lowly in heart" (Matthew 11:29), is able easily to draw near and bless.

Mrs. Jeanne Harper loves music, walking, the out-of-doors and gardening. She travels extensively with her husband, Father Michael, who is the Dean of the British Antiochian Orthodox Church under Bishop GABRIEL Saliba of Paris. The BAOC are the first English Orthodox churches started by converts rather than by ethnic Orthodox from other countries. The Harpers report much interest in the Church, particularly from Anglican priests and laity.

∞ Shannon Gruwell

Never Lose Sight of Me

I was standing before the Pacific Ocean in Malibu, California, the evening before my chrismation. A number of my friends from nearby colleges were at a distance, enjoying a bonfire and catching up on old stories. I could hear them laughing, and a part of me wanted to join the lighthearted circle, but I could not pull myself away from this time of contemplation by the water. The seriousness of the decision I had made to join the Orthodox Church weighed heavily on my heart. I was not necessarily questioning whether I was doing the right thing, but whether I completely understood all I was committing myself to. Making a lifetime commitment at the age of nineteen seemed a bit overwhelming.

It was not that I was rushing into anything; I had taken nearly a year to learn about Orthodoxy. My searching started when I was in high school, much to the surprise of the rest of my family, a number of friends, and the pastor of the church I had been attending. At the time, it was a difficult position to find myself in, knowing that so many people were concerned about me, or even feeling disappointed in the way I claimed God was leading me. My friends and family had always trusted my judgment, but now loved ones worried that I was somehow being led astray. I had tried to explain to these people that I was truly longing to worship God in such a way that the focus was no longer on me and my feelings, but on the Lord to whom I bowed my head in service.

It was on a high school drama retreat at beautiful Lake Tahoe that I first heard about the Orthodox Church. After skiing all day long, the only thing my tired friends and I felt like doing was sitting by the warm fire and talking. During this time, a wonderful theological discussion took shape as we all began to contemplate heaven and the Kingdom of God. We discussed the fact that, in many ways, the Kingdom is here today, and that when we go to worship in church, we are actually worshipping God in heaven. In addition, because we are His children, we are able to receive blessings from God today, not just in the future.

As the conversation wound down, I ended up speaking with one friend who seemed to have intriguing things to say. I asked him what church he went to (curious, since some of the things he talked about were unfamiliar to me), and he told me that he had been going to an Orthodox Church. This was a simple, fleeting introduction, but the longing to know more was planted. We ended our conversation by joking about how if we are in the Kingdom of God today, then there should be no pain even if we were to fall down on the slopes that next day. Little did I know! Early the next afternoon, I went off a ski jump and did not land successfully. I broke my arm in seven places and had to have immediate orthopedic surgery. Even despite indescribable pain, as I was still lying there in the snow, I looked up to the friend I had been talking with the night before and said with a smile, "There is no pain in the Kingdom of God!" Though many around thought I was joking, there truly was a joy in my heart.

The week after my surgery was not quite so full of serendipity! But one good thing that came from my fall was that I had time to read. During the few days I spent home from school recovering, I read a book titled *Becoming Orthodox* by Father Peter Gillquist. It spoke of things that I had often longed to know more about, such as the Church calendar, the intercessions of saints, the meaning of the visible Church and her purpose. I wondered why I had never been taught some of these things that seemed so essential to the Christian Faith.

Since early childhood, I had faithfully attended church with my family, and I always remember having a deep love for the Lord. Our large, nondenominational congregation enthusiastically supported mission and outreach programs. At age seven, I began writing letters to missionaries, telling them that God wanted me to be a missionary too. People would often make comments to my parents about my childlike faith.

As I grew older, my desire to be a missionary remained. At age fourteen, I went on my first summer missions trip to Indonesia. Though I was still very young, I experienced a deepened relationship with the Lord in this environment, as every day I was challenged to live out my faith in God. But when I returned home, I felt suddenly misplaced. I couldn't figure out why I had felt so much closer to God during my disciplined summer overseas.

I still went to church every Sunday and participated in youth group, but I couldn't recapture that same closeness with God. Not knowing how to keep the summer fires burning, I felt that I was failing God. Meanwhile, people praised me for my courage in spending a summer away from my family on a missions trip. I felt I could not let other people see how I was struggling in my relationship with God. I decided I must live up to their expectations, though I wished that someone could see through my veneer of spiritual strength.

Desiring to find that closeness again, I chose to spend the next two summers abroad. I prayed that I would still hear God's voice clearly as I returned home, knowing that my greatest struggle was to remain faithful to God in my familiar setting. The story was the same each summer as I returned home.

Church became a duty rather than a joy, and each Sunday I would come home saddened and discouraged. It was all an act. Yes, the pastor gave encouraging sermons and the music was lively, but still I felt unfulfilled, sensing there was something more to worshipping God than just a weekly inspiring sermon and a few uplifting songs. But I did not know where else to go. This was the church that I was raised in, and as far as I knew as a high school student, the place I belonged.

Remembering the ski trip conversation and the book I'd read, I decided to visit an Orthodox church. (I'd also been thinking about Church history because I had written a paper for my English class on the topic.) The experience of first visiting an Orthodox church is similar for most people, who will often say that before they saw the inside of the church, they could smell it! I was prepared for the incense from my studies, and found it pleasant, like nothing I had ever smelled before. For me, it signified a place of worship, and prepared my spirit.

A deacon handed me a liturgy book and greeted me as I entered the church, feeling awkward at first and unsure of exactly what to do. I heard unfamiliar music, but the words rang with truths from the Bible. Though I did not know the Liturgy, I noticed that much of what I heard was straight from God's Word. Still, I felt I did not belong—there was so much I did not know or understand.

I took comfort in the fact that there were some familiar faces in the church, including some people that I had known from the church of my youth. "It could not be all that bad if these people are here!" I remember thinking. Despite this bit of relief, I walked out that day with more questions than I had had going in. Why do people kiss the priest's hand? I wondered. Why could I not receive Communion? How big a role does Mary play? How do Orthodox people view other churches? I wanted to understand, but as far as I knew this place was not for me.

Yet I chose to go back a few weeks later. My understanding had grown through my studies and I was spiritually hungry. I wanted to see whether it would make more sense a second time around. That second time turned to three, and more, until it became a habit to attend church with my family early in the morning, then quickly drive to the Orthodox church for the Liturgy.

After a number of weeks, my mother and father grew concerned over this Sunday morning ritual. They asked me what I was learning and why I was so compelled to keep visiting. I was excited to share with them all that I was discovering, explaining that I was feeling a bit unfulfilled at our church. More and more, I missed the presence of an historical understanding of the Christian Faith. The church we were in never discussed anything from the Fathers, or recited the great creeds. I said that during the Liturgy I was reminded that I was worshipping not only a loving God, but the Mighty God of creation.

My mother suggested I talk to my pastor, and I agreed. I wanted to make sure that I was not walking down a harmful path, and to share with him about the closeness with God that I was experiencing for the first time since my mission summers. I wondered what he thought about the historical perspective that Protestants never seemed to discuss.

I made an appointment with my pastor, a man I felt close to and respected. Looking forward to our discussion, I hoped he would help me find answers and would feel reassured that I wanted to follow God's will for my life. But when the day finally came for our meeting, our discussion did not last very long. We talked about many things, including Church history, but he cut me off short with very pat answers. He concluded our conversation by saying that if I was looking for tradition and ritual, I might as well go to a Catholic church.

I walked out of his office that day in turmoil. Was he telling me that what I already had should be sufficient? I wanted to believe that, but I had already tasted the wonder of Orthodoxy. I would sit in church with my family and look forward to going to the Liturgy only a few hours later.

Discussions with my parents became more frequent and heated. When I mentioned this to one of the priests at the Orthodox church, he kindly said there was no need to rush any decision, and that my first concern should be to respect my parents. Out of frustration and confusion, I finally stopped going to the Orthodox church, and focused on the fact that it was a blessing to be in church together as a family.

While I was no longer attending the Orthodox church, I continued to pray about my desire to join the Church, deciding I would put off looking into it further until I went away to college. There, I would be free to make more decisions for myself without causing my parents undue concern, and I could ask the Lord to direct me without worrying about the expectations of other people. At the end of the summer, I moved into the dorms at Westmont College (an evangelical liberal arts school in Santa Barbara) as a freshman. Not letting any dust settle under my feet, I visited St. Athanasius Orthodox Church the very next Sunday.

That visit to St. Athanasius seemed like a homecoming. I had waited for the Lord to lead, rather than making up my own mind as to how things were going to happen. Orthodoxy has taught me that this is the best thing for me. Though this was a different Orthodox community from the one I'd visited in my hometown, I felt a deep love for the church and people from the very beginning.

Eagerly, I enrolled as a catechumen and began meeting with the priest weekly. Up to that point, much of my learning about Orthodoxy had come from books and casual conversations with other Orthodox Christians. Catechism was a time to walk seriously through the doctrines of the Church, asking questions and seeking the Lord together. The more I learned, the more I longed to be Orthodox; but as I had been told, there was no rush! My catechism lasted a number of months, and the date of my chrismation was set for January 30.

This brings me back to the night before my chrismation in Malibu, where I stood looking over the water as I began to weep. I longed for Jesus to show me exactly what He wanted in my life, and I did not want to be led astray. I wanted to do the right thing!

Everything seemed to stand still except the chilling breeze from the ocean. I stood in silence, listening. In the stillness, I heard, "Just never lose sight of Me." My tears poured as I closed my eyes and lifted my head. I smiled with relief, knowing the truth could not have been spoken more clearly. I only needed to keep my eyes on Christ, for it is He that I longed to worship, and He that is so glorified in the Orthodox Church. In becoming Orthodox, that has been my constant desire—to keep my eyes on the One who has given me life by His Body and Blood.

I was chrismated the next day, standing with joy in my heart, my head bowed before the icon of Christ. As the people sang, "God grant you many years" at the conclusion of the Liturgy, I could not help but feel that I was looking upon the faces of my brothers and sisters.

It has now been three years since that day. My family and friends have grown more accepting of my decision, as they have seen its good fruit. My father often attends Liturgy with me when I'm home from school, and this gives me great joy. Of course, the day one becomes Orthodox is only the beginning of a journey, and the journey is not easy. My life in Christ has not been perfect—far from it! I have found that loving God cannot be based on feeling good about things, but it is in the Church that I find a way to keep walking when I seem to have no longing to do so. Lord have mercy.

Shannon Gruwell is finishing up her major in English Literature at Westmont College, where she keeps busy with extracurricular activities such as choir and drama. She continues to seek God's will for her life, and prays that others in her life will find the Church.

ᗫ Ann Najar Baumgartner

How Should We Then Live?

Twenty years ago, the evangelical author Francis Schaeffer asked the question, "How should we then live?" in his book of the same name. Many Protestant readers were challenged to live out the implications of Christianity. I was one of those fired-up activists, seeking to transform American society by applying my Christian beliefs to every area of life—the home, the school, church, and my profession.

Initially, my enthusiasm, energy, and drive were boundless. There was just one problem—it didn't last. Despite the intellectual soundness of Schaeffer's teaching, and the validity of his conclusions, I found myself unable to sustain my fervor.

How do you hold on to the euphoria of being newly "born again"? Where does the power to grow in Christ come from? Is Bible study the answer, or prayer? Ministry to the needy, or Christian activism? Evangelism, or small group fellowships? Different Christians suggested all of these possible solutions to me as I struggled to recover the joy of my salvation. But not until I discovered the historic Holy Orthodox Church with its sacramental life did I come to know the real secret of maintaining Christian spirituality.

My father was the son of a Lebanese Druse immigrant. The Druse, a Moslem sect, acknowledge both the Koran and the Bible as inspired Holy Books, and teach that Jesus was a good man. As a U.S. soldier stationed in England during World War II, my father met and married his English bride, my mother.

Although baptized by the Church of England after my birth in Blackpool, I never attended church regularly until I was almost thirty years old. The Druse background of my grandfather powerfully influenced my father's attitude toward Christians—he thought they were all hypocrites. My parents placed little emphasis on church attendance, either in England or in the States, where they moved while I was still a baby. Yet they always stressed morality and values, and I had a strict and disciplined upbringing. I learned responsibility, honesty, and integrity, and I always knew I was loved.

Though we never attended as a family, I did periodically visit a Baptist church. I yearned for a deeper understanding of myself and of the world, and as a youth I delved into philosophical poems and essays on the ultimate meaning of life and the universe. I remember standing on my back porch gazing at the night sky, wondering. How far away are the stars? How long have they been there? How did they get there in the first place? I am certain this God-given wonder influenced me to pursue a physics major in college.

During those college years, I met Bill Baumgartner, and we were married in the Methodist church he had attended as a child, seeing the wedding purely as a social event. We never went to church the first five years of our marriage; we simply were not interested. Or so we told ourselves. To this day, I shudder to think of the gloomy depression I experienced many Sundays, the gnawing fear and guilt for no apparent reason. We lived a comfortable, productive life, but something was missing.

While teaching in a private school, I met several bold, witnessing evangelicals—my first encounter with on-fire Christians. At times, I would spar with them over their beliefs, but one of the local pastors who spoke at an assembly impressed me, despite my doubts, and I suggested to Bill that we visit his church. As it turned out, we began to be drawn to reformed theology through this new mentor, the godly Dr. Cortez Cooper. Eventually, we were won to Christ through his gifted teaching, love for God, and concern for his fellowman.

I thought I had found heaven. I immersed myself in the Bible, and in Dr. Schaeffer's philosophical defense of the existence of God contained in several of his books. Bill read along with me, because they addressed issues that had troubled him. Once he became convinced, he was unstoppable. He read and studied everything he could regarding reformed theology; in fact, he became a kind of expert on the subject of "right doctrine," Presbyterian style.

For several years, the joy of newfound belief, the challenges of learning the Bible, and our involvement in Christian activism sustained our faith and kept it fresh. We spent ten years leading the pro-life movement in the Middle Tennessee area. We helped establish a ministry to elderly, homebound people. Bill taught Sunday School and a home Bible study, which we hosted.

Yet, distressingly, in time we could see all this activity was not saving the world, and in the meantime our own church and denomination were crumbling from within. Our pastor, Dr. Cooper, was devoutly faithful to the Scripture, but that was not true of every Presbyterian. Controversies raged over pivotal issues: absolute truth *versus* relative truth, the sanctity of human life *versus* a woman's "right" to choose abortion, creation *versus* evolution, women's ordination, and even the divinity of Christ. Unfortunately, Bill and I were in the middle of all the controversy. We grew disillusioned, confused, bitter, and rebellious, which in turn led to spiritual impotence.

Inevitably, our church did what seems to be the ultimate result of many Protestant conflicts. We split. A group of us started a new congregation, more to our own liking. We quickly discovered we had only traded one set of problems for another. Having purged our ranks by exiting *en masse*, we now found that the enemy was ourselves. We fought over the details of right theology: predestination *versus* freewill, monthly Communion *versus* weekly observance. We even disputed the teaching methods in Sunday School! Again, Bill and I rebelled, and again, we stagnated. Yet we persisted. We continued to go—to try to worship and to work up the old enthusiasm, but it eluded us.

Bill is an avid reader and student, and somehow he became acquainted with a number of works on liturgical worship. Most of these were written by frustrated, confused Protestants who were themselves trying to recapture what had been lost after the Reformation. Ironically, through a Presbyterian minister we were introduced to the writings of Orthodox theologian Father Alexander Schmemann. Bill immersed himself in these books. I was impressed by Father Alexander's eloquent descriptions of the Eucharist, liturgy, and the sacramental life. Providentially, several of our friends were also becoming interested in liturgical worship. Weary with our bare auditorium/gym/sanctuary and the three-point how-to sermons only as good as the preacher, I was ready to look at another approach.

While we were still reading these books and rethinking worship, some friends invited us to attend an Easter service at a small, Orthodox country church we had always thought of as a fringe group. In fact, years earlier, when St. Ignatius was still part of an independent movement with the hopes of eventually becoming canonically Orthodox, Bill had branded it as a cult in classes he taught. Bill had heard rumors that this church didn't adhere to the Protestant doctrine of *sola Scriptura* (the Bible alone), but instead taught that the *Church* had the right to define the limits of biblical interpretation. These are fighting words to any evangelical Protestant. And so, the first time the invitation to visit was extended, we declined.

A year went by, and again our friends invited us. We were so discouraged by our situation that Bill was going to set aside his reservations and check out this "cultic" gathering—alone. Insisting that it couldn't be any worse than what we had been subjecting ourselves to for the past few years, I firmly told my husband we needed to either go as a family, or stay away as a family. He agreed, and we all went.

My first Sunday at St. Ignatius Orthodox Church was Pascha. What a glorious entrance into heaven! To go from an expensive but stark megachurch, to a humble country church resplendent with icons, rich in color, fragrant incense, ornate chalices and crosses of gold, embroidered vestments, ringing bells, and lilies—my senses almost couldn't take it in. The warm glow reflected by the halo on the icon of Christ, and the angelic voices of the choir singing the Trisagion hymn, lifted me into another realm. The people participated throughout the entire service, with singing and prayers; clearly this was not a spectator event. I resonated with everything, though there was much in the symbolism I didn't understand. Even though it lasted two-and-a-half hours, I hardly noticed the time. The act of standing during much of the Liturgy, along with the total involvement of all of my senses, engaged me and focused my attention on worship. The champagne brunch which followed probably made as much, if not more, of an impression on me. These people were actually going to *celebrate* the Resurrection of Christ! For years, I had tried to feel intensely "religious" about what I knew was the most significant event in the history of the world. But even in my deepest spiritual moments, I never felt I was properly observing Easter. What we did always fell so short of the enormity of Christ's sacrifice. And it would never have occurred to me to celebrate this day with food and drink, as I did other important events in my life. Even to an outsider, it was obvious that the traditional Protestant observance of Easter paled in comparison with the richness of the Paschal Liturgy and Feast.

The warm reception we received from Father Gordon Walker (who was fully aware that Bill had targeted him personally and publicly as a leader of this "cultic" group) encouraged us to return the following Sunday. For the next four months, we split our time between St. Ignatius and our Presbyterian church, but I began longing to partake of the Eucharist with our new Orthodox friends. The communicants truly did seem to be entering into the joy of the Lord.

Father Schmemann notes in *For the Life of the World:*

We have no other means of entering into that joy, no way of understanding it except through the one action, which from the beginning has been for the Church both the source and fulfillment of joy, the very sacrament of joy, the Eucharist.

Today, no matter how deep my feelings of guilt, dissatisfaction, or turmoil, the Eucharist has the power to rejuvenate me each Sunday. I did not understand all of this then, but I sensed it.

While I was won over almost immediately, Bill wanted to understand everything first. He was not ready to relinquish his staunch commitment to Calvinist predestination and covenant theology; furthermore, he was even more reluctant to embrace Orthodoxy's veneration of icons, exaltation of the Theotokos, and belief in Church Tradition as a means of scriptural interpretation. We both spent many hours in discussion with Father Gordon and his wife Mary Sue, who had once been Protestants too. We identified with their experiences and those of others who had converted out of backgrounds similar to ours after a long search for the Church.

Although we spent much of the next eight months struggling with the tenets of Orthodoxy, I began to develop an unshakable conviction that the true roots of Christianity reached back past the Reformation, in an unbroken path starting with the Lord and His Twelve Apostles. I could see that the present patriarchs and bishops could trace their line of ordinations back to the Book of Acts. I began to question the standard Protestant explanation that the Church had lapsed into great heresy for fifteen hundred years after Christ's Ascension, only to be set aright by Luther and Calvin. After all, if the truth of the Faith had been lost for that long, and only just recovered in the past five hundred years, how could it have been recovered by men no different from those who had lost it to begin with?

Then, what had these men immediately done with this rediscovered truth, but to disagree over fundamental doctrines? *Sola Scriptura*, the foundation of the Reformation and of Protestantism itself, didn't make any sense in light of the thousands of existing divisions in Christendom. Each simultaneously claims to hold the proper interpretation of the Bible, refusing to unite in one body due to differences in key points.

We concluded that no one *really* believes in *sola Scriptura*. In our experience, it had always been Scripture, me, and my favorite Bible teacher. Where do we turn for the final understanding of God's Word? We will either choose one of the many Protestant interpretations, our own opinions, or the Holy Tradition preserved by God's Spirit and faithfully transmitted to us over the centuries.

Recognizing this Church to be that Keeper of the Faith answered my intellectual doubts, but it was the call of the Eucharist which compelled me most of all. I was dying of spiritual hunger and thirst, and now knew that no amount of Bible study or church activity would meet these spiritual needs, any more than a good education can help me feel full when I am hungry. The body needs water and food; I needed Christ in the Eucharist.

When we decided to become Orthodox, we met with considerable opposition and disapproval from some family members and close friends. I believe they were hurt and felt betrayed. After all, Bill had spent years indoctrinating many of them in the reformed, Presbyterian theology. It was painful for us not to have them sharing our joy. But trying to explain the full scope of Orthodoxy to someone who has not experienced it is like trying to describe the vivid colors of God's creation to a sightless man. It really is necessary to come, taste and see—to experience it, as well as to learn about it.

Our friends were convinced we were becoming idol-worshippers whose very souls were in jeopardy. Nevertheless, we invited them all when we were chrismated on Great and Holy Saturday of 1991, exactly one year after our first visit to St. Ignatius. It was then, and still is, our deepest desire that those closest to us over the years would also be drawn to the Holy Orthodox Church, and that they too would be recipients of the priestly blessing, "Peace be to you."

How to describe my first real Pascha? I remember realizing that the fasting, penitential period of Lent was the perfect preparation for the celebration of the Feast. I remember the cleansing effect of Forgiveness Vespers, when each member of the parish went, in orderly fashion, to each other, asking for forgiveness for any offense he or she might have inflicted. I found myself doing what I had always been taught all Christians should do, but had never done myself nor seen much evidence of any others doing—fasting, praying, forgiving. I remember the relief of confessing my sins in the Sacrament of Confession, of knowing God's release, and hearing the wonderful pronouncement that my sins were forgiven through the power of Christ.

As I reflect on my youth, I recognize the hand of God directing me in ways I never understood until years later, at times when I gave very little thought to my Creator. I am grateful to that pastor who brought me that next step, into a living relationship with Christ. I am grateful for the many years of sound Bible teaching I received as a Presbyterian; the truths I learned there were eternal. But there is so much more that Protestantism has abandoned, that can only be known through coming back to the Holy Orthodox Church, unchanged for two thousand years.

A teacher at heart, Ann earned her MST from Middle Tennessee State in 1969, before working in both private and public high schools for ten years. For the past twelve years, she has moved the school home and

taught Anne Marie, now married and a student at Rhodes College in Memphis; Rachael, a new collegiate; and William, a junior higher. Her husband Bill is a professional engineer who owns a consulting firm in Brentwood, Tennessee.

∞ Mary Heather Lowe

Against Relativism, Toward God

The roots of my turn toward Orthodoxy can be traced back to the day I came up against the real meaning of the word "relativism." Chronologically speaking, that would be my junior year at university. At that time I was your typical college student, rejecting nothing and accepting anything with bland decadence. The more homosexual or loose friends I had, the more drugs I tried, the more daring the drinking story, the cooler I was, for the most essential attitude of a "Gen X" member is one of jaded cynicism.

Like the rest of my friends, I lived with an eye toward my biography, self-consciously making sure that nothing in my life contradicted the New York pretensions we all shared. Every night had to be above all *interesting*, and that meant collecting experiences. Nothing could be condemned, for who were we to say what was and wasn't wrong? After all, we were smarter than the rest of society. We were in *college*, and our professors had taught us that all the best people were tolerant, open-minded, and accepting of diversity.

Anyone who held to a strong moral code was judgmental, uneducated, and just plain backward. In short, I was in godless, atheistic straits. It's difficult to pinpoint exactly how or why my religious life (or lack thereof) began to change course, but the turn manifested itself in the kind of reading I began to do. Somewhere along the line, the books on my night stand became more conservative in tone and more traditional in content. And in their pages I found that the term "relativistic" was not a compliment.

Two quotes are representative: "Tolerance is an overrated virtue," intoned William F. Buckley, Jr. "One's mind should not be so open that the brain falls out," wrote a caustic G.K. Chesterton. Both remarks struck a chord within me; indeed, they let loose a torrent of long-forgotten beliefs. For I had not been raised to be the kind of girl I had become in college. My parents were not conservative politically, but they had strong values and they taught me the difference between right and wrong. I followed their way of life right up until the age of 18, when college turned me into their photographic negative. This phase, in which I affirmed everything and denied nothing, lasted about two years.

So Buckley and Chesterton snapped me back to a former self. Yet it was actually another writer who changed my mind once and for all. If, as Kafka supposes, a book must be the ax for the frozen sea inside us, the book that served as my ax (as it has done for so many others) was *Mere Christianity* by C.S. Lewis. Lewis put an immediate and sensible stop to my relativistic thinking and reminded me that we *can* in fact say what is right and what is wrong (indeed we must, if we are to assert anything at all), and that the concept of Truth *does* exist.

Furthermore, the book convinced me that Truth was to be found in God. I remember being surprised and a bit disappointed that someone so discerning and wise as myself (ha!) had wound up at the same old answer as so many of my ancestors. I was a bit chagrined. I had expected to come up with something *new,* and the pesky old answer of "God" was all that I had found.

There I was, a 20-year-old who had grudgingly converted from atheism to theism. No love for God filled my heart as yet, but a love for Truth did, and that was a start. Now I needed a denomination. I couldn't very well return to the faith of my parents, as they preferred to believe in God outside of a church setting. Both had had bad experiences with church.

Dad grew up Southern Baptist in the hills of Kentucky, where religious views were held so passionately and blindly as to make their adherents (he felt) un-Christian. Dad resented his sister's rejoicing when we wrecked a new car; we had bought it on a Sunday and she thought that was God's way of correcting us. Neither did he see any Christian love in the Southern Baptist way of excoriating AIDS victims.

Mom, on the other hand, went through three denominations in her youth: Presbyterian, Baptist, and Methodist. The Orthodox Presbyterian Church was much too structured for my strongly independent mother, who rebels against black-and-white conceptions of piety and campaigns for the existence of gray. Her next church, the Baptist, was marred by internal strife, and she remembers the dismissal of her minister as a painful thing. In Methodism Mom felt free to worship as she wanted to; here at last she could "make her own decisions."

She, my father, my older sister, and I attended Methodist churches until about 1980, when I began competing in horse shows throughout the Southeast and weekends became too busy to allow for church. "Once we got used to not going, it was just easier not to go," says Mom. She also grew tired of seeing "so-called Christians" not practicing a Christian lifestyle outside of Sunday worship. As a result, from about the fourth grade on, I did not attend church.

I don't regret this fact. My parents have a lingering guilt about my lack of church training, but secretly I thank them for the way it worked out. If I had been born Orthodox, my young mind almost certainly would have perceived Orthodoxy as rigid and stifling, and I would not be where I am today. I thank God that I was forced to search for my religion, for what is given to one is appreciated far less than what one must work for. Orthodoxy has become my "pearl of great price."

Given my family background, then, it was inevitable that I should try worshipping in absentia for a while. But, of course, I ultimately found such an approach unsatisfactory. If God thought it was okay for us to worship Him without community, I reasoned, He wouldn't have created the Church.

Not that I really wanted to begin attending an actual church. I'd been to more than a few, and without exception I hated the fake community, the false love, the singles' groups, the coffee hours, and the busybody do-gooders I found there. (Misanthropy pervades my nature, and contact with other people is difficult for me.) I despised the tacky representations of a weak-looking Jesus and the saccharine sentiments inevitably posted in the fellowship halls. I had to force myself to attend.

I started with the faith into which I had been baptized, which was Methodism. Attending a Methodist service as an adult was like drinking tepid tea. There was no substance to it. Instead of listening to the vapid platitudes voiced by the minister, I sat in a pew recalling the objections of an anti-church friend: "It's all so *brown*," he said, and the aesthete in me understood exactly what he meant. If I were to embrace Christianity, it had to be clothed in the red of suffering and the purple of noble truth. It had to be beautiful, painful, and real, and I would know it as soon I saw it.

The beauty part of the equation was essential to me. Being more of a feeling than a thinking person, I assess the truth of a thing more easily through my emotions than through reason. Keats sums up my approach: " 'Beauty is truth, truth beauty,'—that is all ye know on earth, and all ye need to know." Having cast aside relativism, I was certain that one and only one Truth existed, and the quickest way for me to find it was through a search for beauty. Early on in life I had struck out on beauty in the terminally ugly Presbyterian and Baptist churches; logically, then, the next place to investigate was in the High Church denominations.

But the Episcopal Church I visited was no improvement. A pastel-yellow "modern" hymnal was the only publication in the pew rack. A goofy guitar chorus led us through several weak songs while the female minister vaguely wandered around the sanctuary. I felt nothing but revulsion and a sense of superiority, which was the first of many clues that I was in the wrong place. Any religion that hoped to snare *me* had to be bigger than I was. Its mysteries had to be impenetrable and ever-unfolding, and inspire in me a sense of awe. It had to bring me to my knees. In the Episcopal Church, I was looking down on religion. It was not even as big as I was. This church was definitely wrong.

Further reading reinforced my impression that the Episcopal Church was as relativistic as my college campus. "You're gay? use drugs? believe in goddess worship? are a radical feminist? Come on in! We're so sophisticated that we welcome everyone." They were ordaining any old person who asked in a kind of drive-through dispensation of "grace," and therefore the grace could not possibly be real.

I moved on.

"Maybe if I look for what's really *old* . . ." I thought. "The multiplicity of churches means someone has to be wrong and someone has to be right. If I trace it back through history, I could find out when people started going wrong."

Regrettably, though, the books I read made no mention of Orthodoxy, and I still did not know that it existed. So my "Tradition-is-good" principle led me only as far as the door of the Roman Catholic Church. This was my last hope, or so I thought. I prayed that Catholics might be the one group who hadn't screwed up God's intentions. The Pope was an obstacle, but I was willing to give him the benefit of the doubt. Maybe he was a mystery—I craved mysteries—and I would understand his role later. I ignored him for the time being and set to work with a catechism book.

I suppose I came close to becoming Catholic, but a friend who was also searching had heard it said that the post-Vatican II Catholic Church was no longer salvific. We went into the reasons why, and I began to see that the Catholic Church was unfortunately prone to changing its mind, and on vitally important points of doctrine to boot. How could a church suddenly decide, in the late 1800s, that Mary was immaculately conceived? Did modern Catholics think they knew so much better than their predecessors? Even more important, what *other* new doctrines might spring out at me unannounced? What old traditions (like fasting) might be eliminated?

The beauty part of my test might be met by the Latin Mass (and even that has virtually vanished), but it was obvious, even to me, that the Truth half was in jeopardy. If humans were allowed to tinker around with the authoritative statements on What's True, then Catholicism could not be the True Church either.

Enter Orthodoxy, after all roads had seemingly been tried and an enormous silence existed in my soul. (I should have realized it was the eye of the storm.) Even before I attended my first Divine Liturgy, I intuitively sensed that Holy Orthodoxy was true, but I did not foresee the obliterating effect it would have on my former way of life. Here was the religion that was bigger than I was, that militantly demanded I recognize the truth and adhere to it, that asked me to change my entire life instead of settling for an hour or two of my time every Sunday.

"Orthodoxy"—its very name, with its Chestertonian, take-no-prisoners ring, appealed to the truth-lover in me. Here was a religion that cost something, and that something was my total participation. I would have to stand up in the very presence of God and actively show Him that I worshipped Him, rather than passively sitting in a pew to receive His Word secondhand. I would have to admit to my sins and repent of them, rather than just sort of hoping they would disappear by themselves. I would have to employ every bit of intelligence God gave me just to comprehend the depth of thought reached in patristic writings. And best of all, there would be no guarantee that I would succeed. Salvation did not come automatically with Church membership.

But back to my first Divine Liturgy. The agelessness hit me as viscerally as did the incense. The exquisite language of the Liturgy, the ancient look of the icons, the seriousness of the call to be real Christians, the solemnity and dignity of the worship—all of these things were signs that I was home at last. But they were external. The Liturgy could have taken place in a garage, with no incense and no icons, and I would have felt the same way. The beauty of Orthodoxy resided in her Truth even more than in her physical characteristics. Her theology was perfect and whole—there was simply nothing with which to disagree!

As I entered fully into the Liturgy and began to participate, I was no longer in twentieth-century America. Neither was I in first-century Jerusalem. I was in the Kingdom of God, where all have "laid aside" their "earthly cares" and devoted themselves entirely to glorifying Him. The saints who were present in the icons were powerful reminders of the rewards of fighting the good fight, and the remembrance of the dead was proof that this religion was not merely another worldly invention. It carried on beyond death, merging seamlessly into the age to come.

There were other ways in which the Orthodox

Liturgy avoided the mistakes of denominational Christianity. The monastics in the parish were reminders of the radical commitment to Christ demanded of all believers. The absence of women from the altar demonstrated that this Church had principles that could not be shaken by public opinion and misguided feminist notions, and that she recognized the strong differentiation of sex roles. Children receiving Communion reinforced the idea that participation in Christ's Holy Mysteries is the single most important act we can perform, and that all who are able should partake.

Since my baptism into the Orthodox Church, I have learned that Holy Orthodoxy is no easy road. "When during the first part of the ceremony you turn and spit on the devil," my priest warned, "you are making an enemy for life." As a catechumen I took his remarks metaphorically, but I have come to find out that he spoke plainly. Life has become much more of a struggle since I have pledged myself to Christ. It's clear the devil realizes what a threat to his existence true Christians are, and concentrates his attentions on them. Every decision I make now seems fraught with meaning, and every action more firmly tied to its consequences. I have been tested in ways I never thought possible. But I cannot go back, and when I look at the situation directly, I see that all the strife only points out that I chose correctly. Christianity is suffering, and the cross is not easy. Even so, Joy remains.

What I say now to converts-in-the-making is that the Orthodox Church is one with all of its priorities firmly in place. The Church knows when to recede into the background and let God do the talking. She knows when to point to Tradition and when to point to the Bible. She understands well that there are many things which are unutterable and inexpressible, and she avoids the scholastic traps which would try to explain such mysteries. In short, she has the grace of the Holy Spirit guaranteeing the gift of Truth, Christ the Logos revealing it to us, and God the Father bringing it all to our faith. I have not been wrong in hoping that truth would lead me to God's home. I pray that I never stop following.

Mary Heather Lowe is a communications professional in the field of law. She lives in Atlanta, Georgia, with her pet beagle, Sadie, and her guinea pig, Elmo. She attends Our Lady Joy of All Who Sorrow Russian Orthodox Church. Her hometown of Summerville, South Carolina, has recently been blessed with the founding of its very first Orthodox temple—Ss. Cyril and Methodius Russian Orthodox Church—and her baptism took place there over Pascha with her entire family in attendance.

∞ Virginia Nieuwsma

California Earthquake

In 1989, I lived through a 7.1 earthquake that shook our house to its foundations. Four years later, I experienced another shakeup—one that would forever reshape what I believe and how I live as a Christian. The first tremors jolted me when some good friends told us their entire congregation was converting to Orthodoxy. "I guess that means you'll have to find another church," I said. To our amazement, they went to catechism classes and stayed on as the church became "St. Stephen."

When they hosted an informational night at their home, my husband Tim went to hear former Campus Crusade evangelist and Orthodox priest Father Jon Braun. Again I was shaken when Tim came home and said he wanted to investigate further. Confused by Tim's interest, I set aside my reservations and joined him in a visit to St. Stephen.

Nothing in my experience had prepared me for the Divine Liturgy. No greetings issued from the platform; there was no platform, but an—altar! I couldn't see the priests and deacons much, since they were facing the front too. This was an adjustment for one used to sizing up the pastor's style and presentation as a part of my critique. When I looked up I saw icons of Jesus, Mary, angels, John the Baptist, and Stephen, somberly looking at me, past me, yet through me somehow. And that smell! Associations with New Age bookstores collided with a vague sense that somewhere, believers of the one true God used incense too.

I glanced at my service book. "How long does this thing go on?" I wondered at its fifty-four pages, especially as I noticed many children quietly participating. Then there was the music—otherworldly and *a cappella*. Its beauty drew me; its strangeness jarred me. I couldn't imagine church without the familiar special numbers and hymns. I found the priest's singing distracting. Couldn't he just *read* that Gospel passage?

"Homily—the sermon," I thought. The priest spoke fervently about following Christ. I relaxed a bit; my churchgoing had been centered on inspiring sermons. But then, I noticed there was more to come. All these pages just for Communion? I wondered. To me, it meant nothing more than a brief time of introspection while the ushers came down the aisle with grape juice and crackers. Here, a procession of solemn men carrying crosses, a gold chalice, and icons came around the mysterious front wall. I felt the perverse urge to giggle, then felt ashamed. I had never been in a church characterized by such holiness and reverence. What did it all mean?

All of my ill-informed anti-Catholic opinions kicked into high gear. I come from a long line of convinced and committed evangelicals. That meant no saints, Mary, confession, prewritten prayers, Church feasts and fasts, liturgy, candles, making the sign of the cross, priests or bishops, icons or "images" of any kind (other than the requisite drawing of Jesus in the Sunday school room). How could all these things have a place in true Christian worship?

On the way home my husband said, "Well . . . if we ever become Orthodox, it won't be because we like the service!" And yet, the effects lingered.

Since moving to California seven years before, we'd been asking the question, "Who, or where, is the Church? Is it just a nebulous entity, consisting of any group of people calling themselves Christians and meeting together?" I'd wondered that even as a missionary kid in the Philippines, when I attended Faith Academy in Manila. There a plethora of groups mingled quite affably, and yet we knew everyone taught different doctrines to the Filipinos about baptism, salvation, tongues, and the gifts, to name a few. We were in an interdenominational mission, and dubbed ourselves "Bapticostals," since our family's church in the States was Baptist and my parents taught at a Pentecostal Bible school in Manila.

Who was right? Did Christ intend for there to be such disparate theologies? I concluded then, and later at evangelical Wheaton College, that I didn't quite fit in any category. Perhaps we couldn't be certain this side of heaven whether the Calvinist or the Arminian perspective was closer to the truth. In the meantime, we all believed in Christ and the Bible as best we understood it, and that was what mattered.

"We have found the true Faith," said the Orthodox Liturgy. Could the truth exist in any one church, whole and unbroken? To me, coming from my background, this claim sounded absurd, even arrogant.

After our move to California, we had settled into a Presbyterian church, hoping to find the same sense of God's holiness and rootedness that we had so loved in our Wheaton congregation. But it didn't take long for frustration to set in there as well. To our dismay we discovered Calvin's church now held to quite different beliefs than it had when he was alive. I was asked to speak on a panel that actually found it necessary to discuss whether or not abortion was wrong! I knew what Calvin and multitudes of Christians before him had believed about the issue. But that seemed of little consequence to these modern Presbyterians.

We began to wonder if even the best evangelical churches stood on the same shaky foundation. Yes, they believed in God's Word, but whose interpretation of it? Who had the authority to define truth? To discipline in case of error? These questions, after our first Liturgy, began to seem like ideas of shattering importance, "the one thing necessary." Where was the Holy, Catholic, Apostolic Church the Nicene Creed talks about, where the *faith* and *teaching* of the Apostles and their descendants was still practiced?

Though frightened by the implications of these thoughts, I began to question the Protestant idea that all the "Catholic additions" to the Faith were distractions or heresies. At this point I might have chickened out, had my husband not been so drawn in, heart and soul. I decided to give Orthodoxy a fair hearing, agreeing out of respect and deference to his leadership to begin attending services regularly. Though I had my questions, I sensed the quiet voice of the Holy Spirit leading me forward. I knew I'd be disobeying God if I turned away without an honest look.

We threw every question we could think of at Father Jon Braun and Father Seraphim (formerly Charles) Bell, the priest at St. Stephen. Father Seraphim, being himself a former Presbyterian minister, had asked all of the same questions. Though we considered ourselves theologically literate, we discovered to our chagrin that we had only foggy notions of what the Church before the Reformation had taught.

There were many surprises. The Church had always taught the ever-virginity of Mary? *Calvin* believed in the ever-virginity of Mary? Prayers for the dead and asking prayers from Christians already departed are written in the catacombs? There had been an ecumenical council that once and for all clearly validated the use of icons? (We knew we had to accept the authority of those ecumenical councils; how could we accept the canon of Scripture chosen by godly men in these councils, then turn around and reject the decisions of later councils?)

During one such discussion, Father Jon said, "If you're looking for the perfect church, you'd better look elsewhere. But if you're looking for God and the Truth, then you've come to the right place." He spoke with such conviction and authority that we kept asking, praying, reading. I devoured books on Church history, learning that the Church had always been liturgical and led by priests and bishops. The mantle of apostolic authority was passed through the laying on of hands, and through verbal and written teaching; in this way Holy Tradition (the living, ongoing voice of the Holy Spirit in the Church) was transmitted from generation to generation.

All of this gripped me—I had been so indifferent to that which had come before! I began to realize how prideful my smorgasbord theology had been—"I'll take a little of this, a little of that"— and how it enthroned me as the chief authority. Eventually, a paradigm shift occurred within me. When my understanding differed from the two-thousand-year-old teaching on baptism, icons, the saints, or liturgy, I began to let the Church's teaching stand in judgment on me, rather than the other way around.

One issue became a catalyst for many others. A seminarian and former Baptist at St. Stephen challenged me to find any significant teachers in the pre-Reformation Church who did not hold to the teaching that the Eucharist was, in some mysterious way, truly Christ's Body and Blood. During my first Liturgy I had choked on the words, "I believe that this itself is Your most pure Body, and this itself Your precious Blood." This was contrary to every sermon I had ever heard on the subject. Now, for the first time in my Christian life, I read the Fathers' writings on the Eucharist. I found overwhelming support for the Orthodox, Catholic teachers who'd always insisted that this is indeed Christ Himself in the elements. I also read very strong language aimed at any who might believe differently!

Looking at the Bible, I wondered how I could have missed something so obvious. I was reminded that when the Lord spoke of eating His flesh and drinking His blood, many of His disciples left Him. It was strong and inscrutable language, to be sure. Yet I wondered. Had I been missing a crucial weapon in my spiritual arsenal? Was this how Christians down through the ages had "received Jesus in their hearts as their personal Lord and Savior"? In evangelical churches people went forward once to say the prayer of salvation. In Orthodox churches, for two thousand years, people had been walking down the aisle every Sunday to receive Christ.

"Christ in me, the hope of glory"—I knew that quote. But my faith had always been so mental, an assent to a set of beliefs. The Passover lamb, the feeding of the five thousand, the verses about people partaking incorrectly of Communion and getting sick over it—suddenly these and many other references resonated with new meaning. I began to yearn to come to this altar (of course! an altar) where, unlike the Old Testament where the priests shed the blood of animals for remission of sins, the New Testament Church broke the bread, soaked it in wine, and prayed for the Holy Spirit to descend.

As I studied Orthodoxy, I faced a second obstacle. Instinctively I sensed that, were we to embrace this Church, virtually every significant relationship would be affected, and I would be wrenched from the evangelical subculture I loved. *Christianity Today* and Drs. Dobson and Swindoll were household names: who were Saint Theophan and Metropolitan PHILIP and Father Alexey?

In a Bible study with my kindred spirits and best friends, I was becoming increasingly uncomfortable with the "we can figure it out for ourselves" style of interpreting Scripture. Passages we were studying shone with new light within the context of the Orthodox Church, and yet I felt I couldn't say anything for fear of alienating the others. These women were my soulmates, my homeschool support team, the mothers of my children's friends. I wished I wasn't sensing this growing distance, but suspected that they felt it too.

When Tim hung a few icons in our dining room, I

thought back to the first time I saw them in church, and I wondered how our friends would respond. Some ventured guarded comments about them, while others studiously averted their gaze from the wall where they were hanging.

Orthodoxy was beginning to pull together all our doctrinal loose ends; in many ways it was a fuller, more complete version of the biblical Christianity we had been taught. Yet those we greatly respected registered reactions ranging from indifference to alarm. What was happening to us? Were we falling headlong into great error? On the other hand, how could they seem so unconcerned, or even opposed to what the Church had taught for all these years?

One friend who had investigated Orthodoxy stated, "Well, I ran into some things I didn't agree with." So had we, but we had learned it was our opinions *versus* the testimony of the majority of Christians who'd lived and died since Christ. We knew the Holy Spirit had brought us to this fork in the road, and we had to decide which way we would go.

God's truth is not relative. I had been taught that since day one, thanks to my godly parents. I was beginning to believe that when Jesus said He would build His Church, He had done it; it was not a matter of preference, of flavors. He had built a Church, and it was my job to find it and submit to it.

Could it be, I wondered, that the Protestant world was erected on a false premise? After all, Christians prior to the Reformation didn't teach the doctrine of *sola Scriptura*, for good reason. Scripture was seen as belonging to the Church, and was of no "private interpretation," as the Apostle said. Within the haven of Apostolic Tradition, the Bible makes seamless sense, and countless fruitless battles over doctrine are avoided. But without that reference point? Today hundreds of sects and denominations all claim Scripture as their only point of reference, and the result is a bewildering array of contradictory beliefs.

And it wasn't as if the Orthodox neglected Scripture; the services and the whole life of the Church grant it the central place. We were encouraged to read Scripture daily, and immediately noticed that it made a great deal more sense in its proper context.

We discovered new friends on our journey too. We met godly "cradle" Orthodox who shattered our stereotypes of nominal Eastern Christians. Though still thankful for my heritage, I began to be less resistant to things not birthed in the West. I remembered with renewed respect how Orthodox Christians had withstood persecution from Moslems and Communists.

Tim and I have been blessed with wonderful pastors. But there was a quality of humility, wisdom, and biblical insight in Orthodoxy that we'd never encountered before. I was amazed at how the deacons and priests were infinitely patient with my criticisms and questions; I had never seen people interested in my soul to this extent.

Watching our kids' response encouraged us too. While initially puzzled by some of the changes, they quickly warmed to Orthodox faith and teaching, unhampered by the deep anti-Catholic biases of their parents. Though children aren't explicitly catered to in Orthodox churches, there is infinitely more for them spiritually, and we could see the good fruit as their hearts responded to God. All of their senses participated in worship, through the singing of the Liturgy, the smells from the censer, and the sight of flickering candles and icons.

Children are treated with real respect in Orthodoxy, as the growing Christians that they are, and are never refused the Eucharist just because they are "too young to understand." We could tell over time that much of our work of educating our children in the Faith was being done for us through the exalted liturgies and prayers of the Church. With great relief we realized that, in this context, we would never have to explain that God was holy, or that the Creeds and foundational doctrines of Christianity really were important. The irreverent, "Hey God" tone we'd often observed elsewhere was entirely absent here, and yet there was no absence of joy or celebration.

Our family began to read of mystics, evangelists, martyrs, the monastics of the ages. "I just wonder," Tim would say repeatedly, "why somebody down the line stopped telling us about these people!" Suddenly, "the communion of saints" was more than just a sentimental, abstract idea, and Christians from Bible times onward became real people to our children for the first time.

As we approached Lent, I was finding equilibrium after this earthquake. Yet there were aftershocks to come—I was heading into what has continued to be my greatest struggle in Orthodoxy, the daily life. C.S. Lewis once said, "Christianity hasn't been tried and found wanting. It's been tried and found difficult." I never knew what he meant until I stumbled over this Rock of a Church!

We left a church with peppy, contemporary music interspersed with skits, friendly interviews, and an inspirational talk. The Orthodox love services, long services. Sunday morning goes two-and-a-half hours if you attend it all, and that's after an hour of Vespers the night before. Feasts and fasts are numerous, with—yes, indeed—more services.

If that wasn't bad enough, the music was often chant and the lyrics seemed ponderous and didactic. How I yearned for the familiar rhyming hymns that had moved me in the past, and were still deeply imbedded in my spiritual memory. Then there were the prayers! The ones in church and in the prayer books were long, full of humility and repentance—and a consistent, serious prayer life was just expected. In addition, the thought of confessing to Christ before my priest scared me half to death.

Though I had struggled with the disciplines of the Christian life before, I hadn't ever had that discipline mapped out for me in the authoritative and corporate structure of the Church. It was clear to me that the Orthodox paid more than lip service to St. Paul's admonition to "work out your salvation with fear and trembling." I wanted to condemn it as legalism, and yet I knew in my heart that I was just looking for an escape. "So what does the fast consist of?" I asked an experienced Orthodox woman. We were approaching Lent, the Great Fast—imagine thinking about Easter two months before it happens! (Once again my ignorance was showing; Christians down through the ages would have been appalled at the thought of approaching Easter without fasting.)

"Oh, the full fast is abstaining from oil, meat, and dairy products," she replied.

"You've got to be kidding!" I blurted out.

But she wasn't, so in the following weeks our family made a few attempts to follow the guidelines, and we learned that it was *hard* to say no to the body's demands. Coupled with increased prayer, the prolonged fast of Lent seemed to intensify spiritual warfare, as sinful tendencies were exposed.

By this time I was learning to trust the Church, finding that she always had good reasons for everything. During Holy Week, the climax of the fast, I began to understand the "why" for the fasting and spiritual struggle. In our comfortable culture, I quickly forget how much I am a sinner in need of Christ's sacrifice. I used to be troubled by all the Lord-have-mercy's in the services; Lent reminded me of just how much I do need His mercy. Where had the awareness of sin been in my life? Without that understanding of my own need, I had never fully appreciated Christ's triumph over death.

Consequently, I had never known Easter joy in its fullness either. Words can't describe my first Orthodox Easter. When we left the Pascha service (who ever heard of a Liturgy that started at five a.m. and ended three-and-a-half hours later?), I knew that for the first time I'd observed Christ's Resurrection the way it was meant to be celebrated. Like everything else I'd encountered in Orthodoxy, it asked more of me, and gave oh, so much more in return.

Earlier in my journey I had sometimes persevered only because my husband was on the road, and I knew God couldn't be calling him without calling me as well. But after Easter something changed, and I knew I could never go back to the Protestant world. I was tired of drifting in a boat cut off from the anchor of the historic Church. I had long recognized my own inability to progress in holiness, and now knew I'd been lacking many of the resources that had nurtured Christians throughout the ages. Above all, Christ beckoned in the Eucharist. How could I say no?

A year after our first Liturgy (one doesn't make this kind of move on impulse!), Father Seraphim baptized our four children; then he and Father Jon anointed us with the holy oil of chrism, as their predecessors have done for two thousand years. "Faith of our fathers," I used to sing in the beautiful Protestant hymn. Now that

I had cast my lot with the Faith of the Fathers, I felt like an orphan who discovers, when she is grown up, that her parents are still alive and eager for her to rejoin the family.

With overflowing hearts we sang, "We have seen the true light! We have received the heavenly Spirit. We have found the true Faith, worshipping the undivided Trinity, who has saved us!"

And we are still singing.

Ginny Nieuwsma makes her home in San Jose, California, where she keeps up with one very nice husband, four busy children aged 3 to 13, five egg-laying chickens, one enthusiastic Golden Retriever, and one imperious cat. She also homeschools her two oldest, Annie and April Elisabeth, reads stories to her preschoolers, Allison and Teddy, and writes and edits for Christian publications.

cs Shelley Hatfield

Windows to Heaven

It was the icon. I was ignorant of its silent influence, working on us even as we were unaware. Silently but steadfastly, wherever we moved, the icons I collected as nice, religious works of art were the witnesses of our journey through darkness towards the light that is Orthodoxy.

I viewed them as aesthetically pleasing—the things that every good rectory should have. My art history background taught me that they were the "flat, primitive precursors of the enlightened artistic period of the Renaissance—in which art glorified man." It is no wonder that their true nature and meaning was not known to me. Nevertheless, because of that very nature, they worked on us, waited for us, patiently.

My husband, Father Chad, and I were known as "High-Church Anglo-Catholics," defenders of the Anglican Church as defined by the Oxford Movement. (This movement was started in England in 1833 by scholars and theologians who aimed to reawaken the Anglican Communion to the doctrine, worship, and spiritual life of the Church prior to the Great Schism of 1054.) All was glorious pomp—complete with smells, bells, and a highly choreographed and elaborate ritual. Every Sunday was a grand production, a staged show, to enrich and inspire the masses. It was no wonder that the congregation commented more on the lovely music than the content of the lessons or the homily. This never set well with me, and I was always searching for a deeper expression of faith. As choir director, I always felt drained by the big productions, rather than fulfilled.

Yet, I reasoned, if only we kept doing things properly and in order, if we remained faithful, somehow the glories of Anglicanism would be revived. It was our duty to fight against the heresies (such as the denial of the Virgin Birth and the Resurrection, and the breaking down of the moral tenets of the Faith) that were raging in the Episcopal Church, and to defend our Anglican heritage. People depended on us.

From the moment my husband was ordained as priest in the Episcopal Church, he began to preach against the false doctrines that slowly but relentlessly chipped away at the foundations of the Catholic and Apostolic Faith within the church. As missionaries in southern Africa, we were aggressive Anglo-Catholic revolutionaries, reviving many who had buried their heads in the sand in silent resignation.

Needless to say, we also became the scourge of the

liberal Protestant wing of the church that was seeking to rewrite Scripture and throw out Tradition. My role as a priest's wife was constantly under attack. I was referred to as a "spouse mouse" for simply holding the same views on the ordination of women as my husband did. I embraced traditional family values and understood the importance of living a spiritual life, and so I was accused of being a traitor to my sex.

We watched as many good and holy bishops, priests, and deacons crumbled under the weight that sent many to early graves, and drove others to the espousal of the heresies they could no longer fight. While discouraged, we clung to our strong convictions that it was our job to stay with the laity and fight the battle.

I remember feeling very angry at those who had already left for the Orthodox Church. How could they abandon us to fight alone? I didn't realize it at the time, but they had simply come to their senses; they knew that there was nothing left to save and nothing left to fight for. Deep down in my heart, I knew this, too, but for a time was too envious and bitter to admit it. And still, the icons remained as silent witnesses to the Truth that we had yet to see.

I became interested in iconography when I had a mid-life crisis at the age of forty. After years of being the reluctant musician, directing choirs and playing the organ and piano, I finally admitted to myself that my heart wasn't in it. God called me into a new artistic realm, and I said "yes," hesitatingly but willingly.

For as long as I could remember, there had been a "little voice" inside me, encouraging me to draw, to paint, to create. Art, not music, was to become my passion. At the age of forty, with no formal art training, I almost impulsively took the plunge, enrolling in a two-year course of study in Graphic Art. I am blessed with a wonderful husband, who has that rare gift of seeing the potential in others, and with his total support, I began my life as a full-time student.

During my final year in art school, I happened upon an article written by an Anglican monk, describing his experiences at an Orthodox retreat center in Pennsylvania called the Antiochian Village. He had gone there to study iconography at the St. John of Damascus Sacred Art Academy, and his article seized me with such interest that I could think of nothing else. I wrote to the monk and asked for further information. Eventually, with the help of some of our generous parishioners, I was on my way to Pennsylvania.

I was awed by the beauty of the morning and evening services I attended at the Village. And of course, in this worship, I finally learned the true meaning of icons. They are not flat, two-dimensional, lifeless paintings, drawn by uneducated simpletons, as I had been taught in my college art history classes. Rather, they are windows to heaven—they inspire and uplift us and draw us into a deeper communion with God. My favorite definition is one that Pavel Florensky wrote: "The Icon exists as the visible manifestation of the metaphysical essence of what it depicts." That's a mouthful, but all he means is that icons help us by visually representing what we know to be true spiritual realities.

I have always identified with St. Peter. I plod along faithfully, and eventually a light clicks on. On the other hand, my husband receives the Pauline experiences of thunderbolts and visions. Yet during my stay at Antiochian Village, something profound and inexplicable was happening, something that almost rivaled Father Chad's thunderbolts. Each morning, I would walk around the camp, faithfully praying the rosary (yes, some non-Catholics do pray the rosary!), and each morning I would stop before the shrine of St. Thekla. I knew nothing about her, but somehow felt compelled to ask for her intercessions. I learned later that St. Thekla, Proto-Martyr, was a follower of St. Paul, and was the first female martyr of the Church. (I eventually took the name "Thekla" at my chrismation. It seemed only natural.)

Very early into my session at the Village—indeed, throughout my stay—I realized the first stirrings of a desire to know more about the Orthodox Church. Could it possibly be the steadfast Truth we had been seeking, or was this merely a brief inspirational moment in a lovely and holy place? Time began to make me suspect the former.

The spiritual and emotional changes I experienced were immediately apparent when I returned home, and surprised me—not to mention my sons and husband! I had found a rest that was almost indescribable, a warmth that grows in the inner recesses of the heart, and works its way to the surface. In iconography, it is the inner Light which shines forth from within the person depicted, not a reflected light from an outside source.

In the weeks following my return from the Village, I tried to hold onto the miracle, but saw it become dimmer and dimmer in my mind as I was once again caught up in trying to survive the daily battles that raged within the Episcopal Church. Longing to recapture what I'd felt in my time away, I thumbed through the yellow pages one day and came across the number for St. George Orthodox Cathedral in Wichita. A kind and understanding priest named Father Basil answered the phone. I asked him if we could come down and see the church, and all was arranged for a meeting that was to change our lives forever.

That meeting was, in and of itself, a miracle. Not only was a bond instantly created with Father Basil (now Bishop BASIL), but also the little Orthodox spark within us began to glow. Our youngest son, Sean, and I would drive down to St. George for services, on the rare occasions that I could get away, and I remember weeping on discovering that *this* was the One, Holy, Catholic and Apostolic Church that the Oxford Movement Fathers had sought, but never fully attained.

I also wept for sadness, for I knew that we, as the family of the Dean of an Episcopal Cathedral, could never hope to be a part of this. To leave the Episcopal Church would mean alienation, total chastisement by parishioners, loss of pensions, health insurance, and salary. It would open us up to an entire host of shattering experiences, too frightening to contemplate. When I was at St. George Cathedral, I felt like a child outside a candy store, looking in, and longing, but knowing my pockets were empty. O ye of little faith!

We kept our longings to become Orthodox quiet, although Father Chad had always been openly positive about the Orthodox Church and her theology. In time, the tensions and divisions became greater and greater. Disgruntled parishioners held secret meetings in an attempt to silence the "mad Dean." In an unholy union with the diocesan bishop, a large contingent arose to oust Father Chad. My husband answered the slanderous charges made against him as honestly as he knew how. In the end he resigned over a false accusation, and a trumped-up charge that was actually canonically illegal!

We had our opening, though not quite the way we'd anticipated. We walked away with our faith intact, although I must admit I was terrified as everything we had worked for was gone. Thirty of the faithful chose to leave the sinking ship along with us. (Someone has said that trying to reform apostate denominations is like rearranging deck chairs on the Titanic!) The people of the Episcopal Cathedral launched another attack in an attempt to keep the straying parishioners; this time, they branded Father Chad a cultist who had been secretly paid by the Orthodox Church to initiate the separation.

Undeterred by the rumors, on January 1, 1994, my family was chrismated and my husband was ordained by Bishop BASIL. Our dear friend helped us through the very difficult days that lay ahead, and we rejoiced that we finally could rest under the wing of a good and holy leader, one truly steeped in the Apostolic Tradition.

Thirty people were chrismated a few weeks later, and at that point we all began taking the steps to begin our growth together in God's Church. With the help, prayers, and encouragement of the people of St. George Cathedral, and the prayers of countless Orthodox parishes, we founded the Mission of All Saints, Salina, Kansas. We held our first service in the chapel of a funeral home!

During that first year as a mission parish, we all experienced the doubt and depression which results from a situation that felt uncomfortably like divorce. Many times my husband and I fought fear over what would become of us and our children, with the loss of our pension and insurance, and generally shaky state of our finances. We would ask ourselves if we were doing the right thing, and always God would reply with abundant mercy and with miracles.

Before making the leap of faith, though, we took the proper steps to insure that we would not be destitute and thrown out on the streets, thereby giving our detractors further ammunition. I immediately found a wonderful job in my field as a graphic artist. Also, there were many of the faithful who were committed to seeing the success of an Orthodox Mission through the difficult days that were to come, and who gave generously of their time and talents.

Our task was simple, really. All we had to do was remain faithful and not let the devil get a foothold. Easier said than done! Yet somehow, through our newfound understanding of Orthodoxy, the task was one of joy, and that joy made all the sacrifices easier to bear.

The next step in my spiritual growth came when I immersed myself in the study of Orthodox hymnology and services. With the help of parishioners who had become Orthodox the year before, we threaded our way through the new music and the different structure of the Divine Liturgy, Vespers, and Orthros (Matins).

Remember the narrow path our Lord always talked about? The Orthodox way of life, I discovered, is not an easy one, but it is ever satisfying. For the first time in my life, prayer has been transformed from meaningless, watered-down repetition, to deep, contemplative, life-changing food. I fall down daily, but now I have the tools which enable me to stand back up and continue moving forward.

I now feel appreciated for my role as "Khouriya"

(the Arabic term of endearment for a priest's wife), and I am ever surprised that I am accepted among other Orthodox for taking this vocation seriously. Yes, trials still exist, but somehow I feel completely armed to handle them. Orthodoxy is the miracle that I have been seeking my entire life. I see Christ more and more in those around me, and can at last let go of the bitterness and pain which were my daily food for so many years.

This is only a little beginning in a little life. I have found the pearl of great price, and I know I would give my life for it. My advice to those still seeking? It is the same that I received from countless others who have left other traditions to become Orthodox: *Don't wait.* We had everything to lose, and found that instead, we gained everything. Dive in, drink deeply of the waters. No longer are we on the outside, longingly looking in; as Bishop BASIL said, "The moment you were chrismated, you became Orthodox, and were truly grafted into the Body of Christ."

Raised in the small mountain town of Evergreen, west of Denver, Shelley had a colorful period in her life as a studio musician and singer/pianist in a rock band! Marriage settled her down, and she and Father Chad served as missionaries in South Africa before taking an Episcopal parish back in the States. Mother to two boys, Shelley divides her time between her family, her role at All Saints as Music Director, and her employment as a graphic designer in Salina.

œ Magdalena Berry

Not an Ordinary Life

In the Brooklyn, New York, of my childhood, many middle-class Jewish families employed women, mostly African-American, to clean the house and mind the children. We called them "maids." Ours was Ellen Steele, a devout Baptist and a singer in the church choir. She had no children of her own, and throughout my life she valued me as her daughter. When I called her up to announce the birth of my second child, a stranger answered the phone. Upon my explaining who I was, she said, "Oh, you're the little girl Ellen raised," and told me Ellen had died suddenly the week before.

The story of my conversion properly begins with Ellen, who I know prayed for me. Indeed, she was the sole witness to my early prayers. I've long forgotten the devotions of my youth, but Ellen told me that once I yelled at her because she interrupted me while I was praying before eating my lunch.

It must have surprised her, because my household was very secular. Our religion was much more of a cultural identity than an actual spiritual practice. A

Passover Seder and High Holy Day services were as far as our observance went. My folks did send me to religious school, where I learned a few Hebrew prayers and not much else. The most vivid memory of my childhood religious life is of that timeless moment in the temple services when the ark of the covenant was opened and the golden, glowing, precious Word, the Torah, was revealed. It never failed to move me deeply, and it was integral to all my later experience of the sacred.

In 1968, my family moved out of Brooklyn, to the suburbs of Washington, D.C. Our first winter there, we took a Christmas vacation, during which our apartment was robbed. My parents were understandably distressed at the loss of their property. My mother particularly mourned her jewelry, which was of great sentimental and monetary value.

I reacted to this with sympathy for them, but also a vehement resolution that I would never become as attached as they seemed to be to material possessions. I felt that "things" were fine to have, but of no ultimate value. It was the spiritual part of life that mattered to me. My intense interest in religious experience began early in my teens. Where it came from (and my folks still wonder), only God and my guardian angel know.

As a young woman in the late sixties and early seventies, I had a smorgasbord of spiritual schools to sample. It was the Age of Aquarius. My high school math teacher espoused the philosophy of Krishnamurti, an Indian metaphysician who came out of the Theosophy movement. My friends and I sat around chanting the Hindu mantra "om"; my notebook was covered with phrases from *Walden*. "Spirituality" was hip. Throughout my high school and college years, I experimented with religious experience by seeking out various gurus and teachers, and reading widely in religious texts. I was also interested in humanistic psychology—particularly in the Gestalt method developed by Fritz Perls at Esalen Institute. I engaged in many social action projects, and among my acquaintances were radical feminists, Marxists, and peace movement activists. I traveled across the country a few times. I went to encounter groups, experimental theater workshops, women's poetry seminars, a week-long intensive retreat at a Tibetan Buddhist monastery.

The underlying motive for these explorations was my conviction that there was more to life than finishing school and getting a job (though I did both). I desired something more than what this world offered me, and had some hazy idea of an "enlightenment" that was readily available—I had only to find the most effective means of obtaining it. However, after a few years, I began to notice that nothing fundamental within me was changing. The disturbing facts were that I was becoming more inept at my relationships with others, and more alienated from myself. I could identify what I thought were my problems, but the solutions seemed beyond my grasp.

In 1975, through the grace of God, a way out of this impasse presented itself. A college acquaintance that I ran into at the supermarket told me about a Christian teaching and service brotherhood. The local members were offering philosophy and Bible classes and holding worship services, both of which my friend regularly attended. I don't think I'd ever before considered Christianity as a path to enlightenment. At that time, I didn't know any devout believers, and my only experience with mainline churches was their use as settings for Saturday night coffeehouses for teenagers. No one in my circle had anything to do with them otherwise. The fact that my friend was making the trip downtown to a dangerous neighborhood to go to church was significant, as she had been a fairly dissolute character, even by college-student standards. So I was intrigued. Surely, if someone could actually *do* what I'd heard that the Gospel commandments specified, than they would be at least on their way to enlightenment!

As it turned out, I was impressed by the people I met at those classes, and the worship services affected me profoundly. Much to my surprise, I confessed Christianity, was baptized, and eventually became a member of that brotherhood. We proclaimed ourselves to be "nondenominational and nonsectarian"—a semimonastic group attempting to live in a way similar to that of the earliest Church. We took vows of poverty, humility, purity, obedience, and service. In an era of free love, drug use, and political activism, we were celibate until marriage, drug-free, and apolitical. We had a common purse, and lived in intentional communities, sharing large houses, eating common meals, following a daily schedule of work and worship. It was a radical change of life for me, and one that I felt called to in a very distinct way. I was 21, and I had given my life over to the service of Christ.

My days were very full. I was active in a variety of social service projects, including the administration of a small family shelter for a Methodist church. I worked with various parishes associated with the brotherhood, as a minister and instructor. I got married.

As my interactions with the larger Christian world increased, so did my need to know how various parts of it defined their faith. I studied Thomas Merton, Dietrich Bonhoeffer, and Henri Nouwen and read widely in other contemporary theologians. I familiarized myself with feminist and liberation theology and developed critiques of them. In all of these activities I sought to define more clearly what it was that I believed, and where I stood in relation to that Truth revealed in Christ and His Church.

Surely it was not with the liberal Protestant churches. My husband came home one spring evening, in Atlanta, Georgia, and told me with absolute astonishment that the Methodist minister with whom he had attended a neighborhood clergy meeting had stated emphatically that "the only thing the empty tomb proved was that the tomb was empty." Evidently she thought the Resurrection was a myth, or at the least, open to interpretation. The more I read, the more I realized that she was not an anomaly. There was no attraction for me in what I perceived as an inauthentic, merely intellectual religious faith, having nothing in it of the fiery confrontation with the living Christ that I sought. Contemporary Catholicism seemed to be a stew of "mystical renewal," with workshops and guided retreats filled with those searching for a more satisfying prayer life; pseudo-Marxists proclaiming liberation theology as the antidote to years of oppression in Latin America; and progressives and feminists who stubbornly fought for the "rights" of women in the "patriarchal" church. None of that was very appealing, either. The Amish and the Bruderhoff communities had a style of life that I could respect and to some degree identify with, but that identification had its limits. Their kind of self-imposed isolation, however comfortable and serene it might appear, was not for one who felt herself thoroughly committed to both spiritual growth and action in the world. The two had to mesh, somehow.

Examining other Christian expressions threw the weaknesses and strengths of my own into sharp relief. I had a fervent faith in Christ and His Mother, but no solid theological foundation. Being "nondogmatic" had meant that there were a lot of vital issues I hadn't consciously taken a stand on. It appalled me when folksy evangelicals talked about the Lord as if He were just like them, only a heck of a lot nicer, but I didn't exactly know why I had this reaction. I deeply mistrusted the liberation theologian's "preferential option for the poor." It seemed to me that economic injustice rectified would not result in any net gain in human virtue, and didn't the social reformers' concentration on *this* world serve to distract everyone from that which no power or principality can take away—the love of God?

In a more personal sense, I was coming up against a certain flatness in my spiritual life. None of the materials I had available to me gave me the tools to deal with the demands of marriage, family, work, and community, as they relentlessly presented themselves. My husband and I observed that as single people, traveling lightly through life, we could pack our possessions in one trunk apiece. Marriage somehow got us out of two trunks and into a small U-Haul. And children! Make that a mid-sized U-Haul and pack it tight. Setting up a household involved me in a host of mundane concerns that I had to a large degree been able to avoid before. (I now know that *three* things are inevitable—death, taxes, and laundry.) Nurturing a marriage took time and energy that I had previously taken for granted. A full-time job, volunteer work, and parish committees made for a busy life, and I needed spiritual nourishment lest I get caught up in daily affairs while my interior life diminished.

When my first baby was born, I realized that a

whole new realm of temptation, as well as joy, had opened up before me. What facets of my soul would be exposed in the raising of this child? Did I have the kind of faith and confidence in God that would withstand my baby's injury or death? This was crucial to me. As an adolescent obsessed with the Jewish Holocaust, I had collected stories of those individuals who, despite their sufferings and the hell surrounding them, had maintained their relationship with God. This was the kind of connection with Divinity that I sought. I knew that I was vulnerable to great fear and despondency as a result of my natural loving attachment to my baby, and that my faith would be tested.

Certainly, the Holy Scriptures were there, but I sensed the need for more instruction and understanding. I had reached another impasse. In sum, I knew what kind of Christian I was *not,* but what kind I *was,* was not at all clear. I was deeply dissatisfied with the modern *zeitgeist*—the spirit of the age, especially as it was reflected in the contemporary churches. I wanted an authentic Church, perfumed with the scent of heaven, enriched with profound wisdom concerning the human condition. It was an act of Grace that brought me to the gates of the Orthodox Church.

The advent of Holy Orthodoxy into my life came in the surprising person of a Russian-born monk. We invited him to our parish where, in a week-long marathon, he outlined the history of the Church, impressing us with the majesty of its Tradition, and immersing us in prayer. It was strange and wonderful, indeed. I loved the prayers, the incense, the icons. The sense of holiness was everywhere in evidence in the service books, and a treasure was revealed in the lives of the saints, and the writings of the Fathers and Mothers of the Church. I began reading *Unseen Warfare*, a classic work of Orthodox spirituality, which for me was that rare and precious gift—a life-transforming book. Here was the profound understanding of my nature, and a way of living that could actually enable me to draw closer to God!

For one whose entire adulthood had been directed toward serving Christ and His Church, only Holy Orthodoxy—far more than another set of beliefs, but an entire way of life—would answer. While I have failed miserably at fulfilling the Gospel commandments, their fulfillment has been the axis around which my life revolved. The Orthodox Church as it was revealed to me through the prayers, the sacraments, the teachings of the Fathers and Mothers and the lives of its saints, is the most complete expression of, and school for, the practice of virtue and pursuit of holiness.

Recently, an acquaintance at work asked me if I was interested in "spirituality." She could well have been asking if I was interested in Labrador retrievers—as if spirituality were something one would pursue as a hobby. Orthodox Christianity does not make a distinction between religion and spirituality. Furthermore, "spirituality" is not optional—it's the way you become a fully human being.

There was a price for all of this, however, and while I quickly knew that I would have to become Orthodox, my full conversion took about a year. Seeking entrance into the Church meant that everything about my life had to change. It wasn't a matter of becoming a catechumen solely by going to classes over a period of months, and receiving baptism and chrismation at the end. My catechumenate included abandoning a large part of who I thought I was.

At the time of my introduction to Orthodoxy, I was an ordained minister in my church, and happy to be one! I used to complain to my husband about problems in fulfilling "my ministry," and he'd reply with something like, "Isn't it enough just trying to be a *Christian?*" I'd always say, "Yes, but . . ." I didn't understand him until I started to be taught by the Fathers. As I began to encounter the wealth of Orthodox spiritual literature, I saw what a lifetime's work it was to be fully alive in Christ. Any doubts about my reason for being, or what God's will for me was, vanished.

Only when I had this understanding was I able to "let go" of my chosen profession and see "my ministry" in the context of a fully Orthodox life. God needs workers. Whoever is willing to use his or her gifts in His service can find plenty to do. The trick is to be willing to do what is needed, not only the jobs we think are appropriate, or fair, or in some way deserved.

There were other issues as well. Coming into the

Church through the Russian tradition brought to mind my ancestry in Minsk and Pinsk, in Belarus. I envisioned my grandparents spinning in their graves at the sight of their flesh and blood adopting the faith of those cursed Cossacks they had fled from. However, I'd already made the big step of conversion to Christianity, and in order to do that I had to separate the faith from its supposed practitioners. Indeed, one of the factors in my conversion was the knowledge that slaves in this country had become Christian despite the fact that their masters espoused faith in the same Christ. It seemed to me to be proof of the authenticity of the Christian revelation, that the sufferers would find sustenance in the religion of their subjugators. So I could deal with historic Russian anti-Semitism, knowing that while it may have flourished in Russian Orthodox society, it was not intrinsic to the Holy Orthodox Church. I believe, as the slaves did, that the Church is the fount of salvation for all, regardless of the fallen state of some of its earthly representatives.

Many women, upon encountering traditional Orthodox Christianity, are put off by what they perceive as its "sexism." I was spared this reaction, perhaps because I was so disgusted by my readings in feminist "thealogy." I agree with what Mother Teresa told the World Conference of Women—that men and women are not the same, and we shouldn't try to make them so. I have found that my femaleness is fully honored in a Church which rejoices in the fact that before the Mother of God, philosophers are made fools and orators become as dumb as fishes (to paraphrase an Orthodox hymn). When the presence of the Queen of Heaven permeates our life in the Church, the strength and dignity of women are maintained.

However, I am not particularly concerned with gender-related issues. While we must certainly attempt to discern between the Tradition of the Church and traditions of men, my greatest liberation has come through realizing that the only thing I need be concerned with is a "good defense before the dread judgment seat of Christ."

Mine is a mixed-race family, and I'm occasionally asked if it's difficult raising our children in a racist society. My response is that the real challenge is raising Christian children in a post-Christian world. Being Orthodox means not "going with the flow." It means acknowledging that you're not "o.k.", asking for mercy, and being willing to receive it and repent. It is a constant struggle to remind ourselves and our children of what is really important—not, for example, the immediate discomfort of fasting and standing in church, but the exaltation and solemnity of prayer in the Presence of the Body and Blood of Christ.

Being Orthodox means that there are mysteries that cannot be explained away—that there is suffering through which we must continue loving, and being loved. Being Orthodox means that we are joined in church by a great cloud of witnesses who have gone before us, and whose images in the icons console us, even when the temple is too hot, the singing is off-key, and the babies are drowning out the chant. My children know that they are part of something very special and important, and for that I am grateful.

My life since I became Orthodox has been filled with all the ordinary things—taking the children to school, going to work, keeping on top of the house-cleaning, helping my husband with the parish, births, deaths, pilgrimages. I do a little writing, and get involved in missionary projects. But it is not an ordinary life—it is touched by that scent of heaven that the Church imparts, and it is blessed.

When my little girl asked a while ago, what was the best thing that ever happened to me (probably hoping that it had something to do with candy, or a doll, or both), I replied from deep within, "I was baptized Orthodox." In the Church, I found the "meaning" that I had sought from my youth. Glory be to God.

Magdalena and her husband, Father Moses Berry, live in St. Louis, Missouri, with their two children, Elijah (9) and Dorothy (7). Father Moses pastors Christ the Good Shepherd Eastern Orthodox Church. Magdalena works full-time as a church administrator and is involved with Orthodox publishing.

∞ Lin Richardson

Blessed Are the Pure in Heart

"Blessed are the pure in heart, for they shall see God." For years this beatitude both disturbed and perplexed me. It seemed an impossibility, this purity of heart. I'd realized this much: one certainly could not obtain this intellectually. Yet in my evangelical circles, it seemed that those around me taught that one would become pure in heart if one only gathered enough biblical knowledge.

Over twenty years ago, my husband Bob and I moved from a Methodist church to a fledgling Bible church that was all of six weeks old, and boasted about thirty people. Over the next sixteen years this group became the largest Bible church in Little Rock, with two-thousand-plus adults attending each Sunday. We were in the thick of it, as Community Group leaders and Learning Center teachers. I led women's fellowship groups and taught at retreats. During nine of those busy years, we also worked with an interdenominational Bible study group called Bible Study Fellowship.

With all this intellectual involvement, continuous

Bible study, and activity, one might wonder why I wasn't spiritually content and why I still had no answer to such questions as how to become truly pure in heart. Nonetheless, in the years before we discovered Orthodoxy, I was becoming very distressed over the dryness in my life. My husband and I talked frequently about our feeling that we had reached a plateau in our spiritual lives.

During the regular "how-to-behave" lectures which constituted the bulk of most worship services, I found myself actually tuning out, exhausted by an intellectual faith that wasn't connecting with my heart and soul. Yes, we were adding to our data bank of Christian information, but we weren't worshipping God in our deepest being, and we weren't learning how we might actually be united to God. We even talked about changing churches, but in our area, that meant either the Baptist church or another Bible church—both parallel moves with no foreseeable improvement.

Then, in God's providence, our oldest son Timothy went off to Wheaton College. Ironically, there in the bastion of evangelicalism, he developed a close friendship with a young man named Joshua, the son of an Orthodox priest. This young man began taking Tim to his church, and together they met and studied with the parish priests.

When Tim called home, we could tell he was excited about what he was learning. Our son had never been happy at the evangelical church we attended in Little Rock, perhaps partly because he and his brother Scott had always attended Lutheran or Catholic schools growing up.

When Tim began telling us about Orthodoxy I kept an open mind, but questioned him closely about the Church's teaching. I asked all the unoriginal, standard queries. "Do they worship Mary? Do they worship icons?" Timothy wisely sent me a book by Orthodox theologian Alexander Schmemann *(For the Life of the World)*, saying, "Mom, this is the C.S. Lewis of Orthodoxy." Many of my fears were alleviated as I read, and my heart warmed to this teaching as it hadn't warmed to anything for years.

In the meantime, Timothy moved to Minneapolis to finish his degree in chemistry at the University of Minnesota. My husband and I decided it was time to visit Tim, not only to see him, but to check out the Orthodox church he was attending there. We admitted it: our conversations with our son and the books he sent us had piqued our interest.

And so it turned out, for this Southern woman, my first experience of Orthodoxy was at St. Mary's (OCA) Church, all the way north in Minneapolis. When I walked in, I thought the interior was stunningly beautiful, filled as it was with icons and an ornateness that carried with it a sense of the sacred. Though with the incense, chanting, and constant singing the service was very different from my regular Sunday morning, I felt I was experiencing a sense of reverence and worship that I had never known.

As I sat with this unfolding, I began to notice that the content of the Liturgy was filled with humble prayers and Scriptures worshipping God. Tim had told me that his church was in the Russian tradition. It came to me that all the Bibles and all the service books could be taken away by a tyrannical government, but God could still be worshipped with only a priest and the people, if their hearts were filled with this Liturgy. Indeed, I could see how God had preserved his people despite the horrors of communism, through this worship of the heart.

Toward the end of the service, as people went forward to partake of the Eucharist, I noticed a young man holding his daughter, who was stricken with muscular dystrophy. Her movements were so spastic that he was having a difficult time holding on to her. At the cup, the priest and deacons helped the father and the child with great gentleness and concern, as they very carefully gave her Communion. Never had I seen anything like those men, so focused on this precious little one of God. I knew then that something was very different here, in all this reverence, beauty, humility, and kindness. I was moved to tears, and with joy I desired to know more.

Upon returning to Little Rock, my husband and I started attending the Liturgy at Annunciation Greek Orthodox Church. We were greeted warmly by the

congregation, even though the Liturgy was split between Greek and English. Bob was determined to go to
this church, but I was nervous, not knowing a soul, and
conscious of the drastic differences between my old
evangelical services and these Orthodox Liturgies. I
was in culture shock, but I had never seen Bob so drawn
to anything, and I knew that I could follow him almost
anywhere as long as he could show me that Christ was
there.

So I willingly took the next step. I accepted Father
Elias Scoulas' invitation to come study Orthodoxy with
him once a week. Father Elias is a man of gentle spirit,
vast knowledge, and infinite patience, and he dealt
kindly with Bob and me as we grilled him with all our
questions built up over years of analytical Christianity.
"Question all, and back up everything with Scripture,"
had been our motto. He dispelled our fears, and helped
us understand the importance of the Eucharist, and
why it, rather than a sermon, had always been the
center of Orthodox worship. Actually, we were impressed, realizing he was undisturbed by our questions. *He* was the one backed by the Church Fathers
and the saints, and his Church was almost two thousand years old. All our questions had good answers,
sometimes answers that had been given many generations ago.

Through participation in the life of this church, we
began to break through the spiritual glass ceiling that
we had come to in our evangelical faith. We also realized that we had stopped measuring one another. Was

I a good enough wife? Was Bob manly enough? Was he the spiritual leader of our home? Were our children living up to the standard? We were gradually relaxing into a greater sense of acceptance of each other, and a greater appreciation for the way God had made us. I think that was happening because we were becoming less focused on ourselves, and more focused on God.

After ten months of worship and study, I was very ready to join the Church and begin receiving the Eucharist. With anticipation, we set the date for our chrismation. Bob and I, and our youngest son Joel, would be chrismated on November 21, 1992.

On November 14, a week before our chrismation date, Bob went fly-fishing on the Little Red River. About four in the afternoon, a couple found him, dead of a massive heart attack at the age of fifty. I shall never forget the scream that came from within me that night, nor the look on Joel's face when I told him his father was dead. Bob was a wonderful, godly man, loved by everyone who knew him. I loved him more than life itself. I was terrified.

When Father Elias came to our home that night, my thoughtful eleven-year-old son asked if his father could be buried in the Orthodox Church. He told our priest that his father had loved Orthodoxy and would want this very much. Father Elias gently told Joel that he would have to ask the bishop, since Bob had not been chrismated.

The very next day, on Sunday, Father Elias came back with the answer from Bishop Timothy. "Of course he may have a funeral in the Church," he had said. "Bob was Orthodox in his heart, and he had received the greatest blessing of all, chrismation by Christ Himself." I could not have heard sweeter, more uplifting words. This ancient Church, while heavy with the traditions of the saints, was also steeped in the love and mercy of God. Once again I saw the compassion and tenderness of Orthodoxy.

Joel and I were chrismated the following Sunday. As Father Elias anointed us with the seal of the Holy Spirit, I felt as if someone was touching my hair. Was it the Holy Spirit, or Bob, or an angel, or simply the breeze? I do not know. I only know that I put my arm around Joel, and felt that with the help of the Orthodox Church, we were going to survive.

Yet in the months that followed, my whole life seemed to have burst into flames, and an enormous black hole of hot pain lay in the midst of every moment. Never had I needed God so desperately. It was here, in my rawest moments, as I begged for release from the hideous throbbing one experiences at the loss of a loved one, that my heart was exposed to the healing energies of God. Through what the Orthodox call "noetic prayer," prayer of the heart, I came to understand that we *can* know God. Paradoxically, my deepest despair was also the time I began to experience the reality of that long-elusive beatitude, "Blessed are the pure in heart."

While my mind languished in a thick fog, my soul and spirit were acutely alive with the hurt of Bob's loss. The beauty of the Orthodox services soothed and healed my soul, uniting it to the peace and grace of God's loving mercy. Instead of facing a service of a few choruses, followed by a lengthy sermon that I'm sure would have been of little help to me, I was given the gift of singing the Psalms and prayers of the Liturgy. I drank in the reality that by death, Christ has conquered death, that I could enter into His Resurrection life through faith, fear, and the love of God. In my mourning, I was comforted.

For years I had intellectually offered myself to God. Now, because of the determination of my husband, and my willingness to follow him, the Orthodox Church has shown me the way to offer not only my mind, but my soul to God, who cares for me and loves me. There are no three points and a conclusion; no how-tos. There *is* a way to purify my heart and soul on a lifelong path to the Holy, Triune God.

"Blessed are the pure in heart, for they shall see God." At last I'm beginning to see.

A reader and chanter at her church, Lin works during the week as Director of Practice Management with the Baptist Health System. She has three sons, two of whom have flown the coop, but Joel and her English Springer Spaniel, Holly, keep her company. For fourteen years she has served as a board member for the Central Arkansas Crisis Pregnancy Center.

∽ Mary Vaughn Armstrong

A Time to Listen, A Time to Hear

"Here's something you should read . . . the author isn't an Episcopalian, but his questions sure sound a lot like yours!" I reached for the book my friend Ingrid offered, hoping I looked more interested than I felt. The last thing Bob and I needed was another how-to manual about reviving the Episcopal Church.

"We got it last summer at our granddaughter's wedding," she continued. "At an Orthodox Church in Ben Lomond, California . . . the most beautiful wedding we've ever seen." I thanked her, put the book on the floor beside my purse, and forgot about it. My husband and I had promised each other we wouldn't allow our ongoing theological laments to lead our Bible study group off track one more time.

Heading home two hours later, we talked briefly about tonight's study of Isaiah. Bob's hands gripped the wheel as our headlights cut through wisps of November fog hovering around us. Miles of dark, moonless road stretched ahead, and I remembered our friend's book buried under our Bibles. I dug a small red flashlight out of the glove compartment and beamed it on the cover. "Becoming Orthodox," I read aloud. "A Journey to the Ancient Christian Faith . . . by Peter E. Gillquist."

I skimmed the table of contents. "Listen to this— Part One is called 'From Arrowhead Springs to Antioch'!" I didn't have a clue about where Antioch was. But if the author meant Arrowhead Springs, California, I knew it well. My family and I had spent years in the San Bernardino mountains towering above it—I as a school nurse, my husband commuting to and from his office at Riverside City College. Turning the page, I began to read out loud in earnest.

When we pulled into our driveway the flashlight had almost given up, but I didn't stop reading until the garage door thumped shut behind us. Usually eager to unfold his six-foot-four frame, Bob turned off the motor and listened, fingering the keys as we finished Part One.

We were up an hour early the next morning despite a grey drizzle. Now it was Bob's turn to read, and he opened the book to Part Two: "Orthodoxy and the Bible." As I waited for him to begin I felt like a little girl again, skidding my bike to a stop on California Street in Santa Monica. I'd prop it against the thick trunk of one of the dozens of palm trees that lined the wide street and walk towards the massive Roman Catholic church just beyond, trying to look as if I did this all the time.

I'd climb the steep marble steps, the California sun warm on my back, and walk into the cool shadows of the narthex. Finally I'd slip into the back of the silent church, drawn by its beauty as iron drawn by a magnet. Far down the aisle and to the left, rows of blue candles flickered on an angled stand. I didn't know what they were for, but I loved to look at them. Sometimes I knelt, copying the few people scattered through the church, and looked up at Christ's statue above the altar.

I never stayed too long. We were, after all, Presbyterians. "Our ancestors came to America to get away from that sort of thing," my Scotch Presbyterian mother explained. Several blocks to the west our own church stood tall and regal, where in front of the whole congregation my sister and I sang "Oh Come, Little Children" one Christmas Eve when we were very small. I treasure many memories from our church, like the pot of bright pansies presented to every child on Easter morning, and my classroom's circle of small chairs in rainbow colors. But more than anything else I remember the words of Miss Bacon, my Sunday school teacher. "If we listen," she solemnly told our third-grade class, "we can hear God's voice." From that day on, I listened.

Always, I'd felt different. Not on the outside, as the oldest of the three children born to my pediatrician father and nurse mother—children taught to arrive at the dinner table prepared to contribute to the conversation, ready to discuss issues and events. I felt different on the inside, pulled since earliest memory by a yearning to follow God, to walk with Him, to please Him.

Above all, I longed to worship Him. As I grew up I continued my secret visits to the Catholic church, drawn by a hunger I could not define.

"Where's Mary?" my little brother once asked my father during a family vacation in the mountains.

"Probably praying!" my father laughed, only half-joking.

I laughed with them, but understood. The glue of truth held the joke together.

I attended nursing school in San Francisco, where for the first time I heard personal testimonies by a Campus Crusade group who visited our dorm. Embarrassed by the emotion I felt, I retreated to my room on the sixth floor, knelt beside my bed, and in a whisper asked Jesus Christ into my life. At that moment of deep commitment He became, in a whole new way, my personal Lord.

On Sundays, when I wasn't working, I attended the Presbyterian church two blocks from the nursing school, warmly welcomed by the minister, Dr. Long, who always wore a fresh pink rose in his lapel. I especially liked the candlelight Wednesday evening prayer service, where I learned to pray aloud for my patients— like Mrs. Allen, who had given birth, one by one, to four perfectly formed stillborn babies.

Morning and evening prayer became an essential ingredient of my daily life. I memorized dozens of Bible verses. But something was missing. Then one morning I accepted a classmate's invitation to visit San Francisco's beautiful Episcopal Grace Cathedral on Taylor Street.

In silence I knelt under the soaring arches as magnificent music bathed my soul, and watched the faithful file forward to receive Communion. On the way out I gathered a purseful of material to read. Two years later, I was confirmed by Bishop James Pike at St. Andrew's Episcopal Church in Oakland, California.

It was a compromise acceptable to my Presbyterian family and to me—a blend of majestic liturgy with more Bible reading than I'd heard at one time in any church. The Episcopal Church shepherded me through the years that followed, repairing the jagged pieces of my life when my first marriage shattered, and helping me as I buried my middle son Christopher after a bitter four-month battle with leukemia. Later, it guided Bob and me through many of our twenty-seven years of marriage.

Not long after my confirmation, Bishop Pike had announced his intention to communicate with his dead son, and headed for the Judean desert to do so. Back then I had been too busy navigating the swift currents of my own life to think much about it, but felt ashamed that he was an Episcopalian. After his untimely death in 1969, the church remained calm on the surface, with few aware of the sea change convulsing at its deepest levels. It erupted once and for all in 1976, when the General Convention voted to ordain women as priests, severing almost two millennia of apostolic tradition.

Inevitably, twelve years later a woman was made a bishop by an Episcopal Church in Massachusetts. As though determined to construct a theological house of cards, the Church stacked one innovation on another. It refused to demand clerical monogamy, winked at the reality of Christ's Resurrection, waffled on abortion, and scrambled to create liturgical blessings for unmarried or same-sex unions. A friend, discovering that her son and his girlfriend lived together, mourned, "They keep a book on their coffee table by your church's Bishop Jack Spong—saying unmarried sex is okay, as long as it's monogamous!"

No longer sure where we belonged, Bob and I visited one church after another when we moved to Spokane, Washington. More than a year later we discovered traditional Holy Trinity Episcopal Church. For several years we worked alongside most of its members to restore historic, patristic teaching and values, especially through the Episcopal Synod of America, or E.S.A.

When we moved to Western Washington eight years later to be nearer our exploding population of grandchildren, our priest at Holy Trinity, Father Robert Creech, told us we'd have three choices: find a traditional Episcopal church—rare in Western Washington; convert to Roman Catholicism; or investigate the ancient Orthodox Church. Eager to get back to work, we ended up at another Anglican church.

As Bob at last concluded the final pages of *Becoming Orthodox*, pale November shadows stretched far into our living room. For several minutes we said nothing, until I exploded in excitement. "Where have we been?

All I ever knew about Orthodoxy was from history book pictures showing churches with funny roofs!" We laughed together. "Evidently there's more to it than unfamiliar architecture," Bob answered, standing up. "Think I'll check the Yellow Pages . . ."

The next morning I tiptoed around the kitchen, straining to catch every nuance of Bob's relaxed conversation with Father James Bernstein, pastor of St. Paul Orthodox Church in Lynnwood, the closest parish. When he hung up I quizzed him mercilessly, consuming every crumb of information. As promised, two days later a large envelope arrived, containing, among other literature, a booklet titled "Orthodoxy: Jewish and Christian," detailing Father James' own Jewish background and conversion to Christianity.

Thanksgiving was only a week away, and eagerly we made plans to attend a special Thanksgiving Eve Vespers at St. Paul. At that time we lived forty-five miles from its temporary meeting place, a tiny chapel rented from a Catholic church. We arrived a few minutes late; through the closed doors we recognized the censer's metallic rhythm, but were utterly unprepared for the beauty we encountered beyond.

Tiny candles in red glass holders cast flickering shadows over four large standing icons behind them. The sweet scent of incense hung over the room as magnificent prayers, some familiar but most new, filled our hearts and minds. Much too soon, it ended. Out in the hall we lingered by the bookstand, not wanting to leave, warmly greeted by Father James, Deacon

Thomas, and many members of the congregation. Driving home we wore out two flashlight batteries for the second time in a week, devouring one pamphlet after another.

In the days that followed we read constantly about Orthodoxy, almost afraid to believe such a treasure existed. We discovered a Church nurtured by the Holy Spirit, not only through desperate persecution, but through the faithful, everyday lives of its people. Over and over we wondered why we had known so little about it. We subscribed to AGAIN Magazine, accompanying our check with a short note to its managing editor, Deacon Ray Zell. To our amazement he sent us a return note saturated with kindness, a prevailing characteristic, we discovered, among Orthodox clergy.

Though we couldn't attend Sunday liturgy due to commitments at our Episcopal church, we drove to many Vespers services. In that year, 1992, Christmas fell during the week, presenting to us the best of all gifts: a chance to attend our first Divine Liturgy on Christmas Day.

It was dark when we left for St. Paul, nibbling fruit bread and tangerines as we drove through the empty streets. We arrived at the tiny chapel early, found a place and stood silently before the altar, waiting. Incense blended with the scent of the fresh spruce and pine boughs which decorated the window sills, altar steps, and every corner of the room. At last Father

James' voice, reflecting his rabbinic heritage, soared above us: "Blessed is the Kingdom of the Father and of the Son and of the Holy Spirit, now and ever and unto ages of ages . . ." Together we bowed low before the altar, slowly crossing ourselves in a depth and purity of worship I had searched for all of my life. Without a word, we both knew we were home at last.

Bob and I moved ahead deliberately, carefully, resolved that each step we took should conform to the teachings and traditions of the Orthodox Church. With sad finality we completed commitments to the North Puget Sound chapter of the E.S.A., which we had helped found. I taught my last Sunday school lesson to a class of pre-kindergartners that included our two granddaughters. With equal care we explained our departure to the Episcopal friends we had worked beside and grown to love. Six months after our first Christmas Day Divine Liturgy we began regular Sunday worship at St. Paul, and became catechumens a few weeks later. We soon moved to a house only half an hour from the church, allowing us to come to nearly every service.

For ten months we attended weekly catechism classes at the Bernsteins' home, counting the days between them. Each session began with half an hour of refreshments and talk with Father James' wife Bonnie, their three children, and a dozen or so other seekers. Following the fellowship we moved to their living room, where for another hour we soaked up Father James' careful, methodical teaching on every aspect of

Orthodoxy, recording each class for further study. We glimpsed the reality that becoming Orthodox meant a whole new way of life. With great joy we learned of the Church's adherence to apostolic teaching and doctrinal purity, struggling always against cultural accommodation and innovation. We marveled that Orthodox Christians today believe exactly what the Church has taught since its first-century beginnings.

During this time of learning, each of us selected a patron saint. I chose Mary, the Mother of Christ, whom I had always loved. Bob chose St. Robert of Blois, a French abbot who died in 1011. Daily we invoke their prayers for our adult children and their families, who observe our new lives with guarded interest.

On Christmas Eve, 1993, St. Paul moved into its new and permanent temple on a grassy hill in Brier, Washington. Our chrismation followed on Holy Saturday, 1994, a year and a half after our discovery of Holy Orthodoxy. On that beautiful night incense drifted through the church, white carnations and satin ribbons circled the thick candles we held, and rose petals crunched underfoot as we followed Father James around the Resurrection icon—the first steps of the most glorious journey of our lives. Soon afterwards we received our first Holy Communion as Orthodox Christians, fulfilling beyond all expectation the earliest longings of my heart.

Before dawn the next morning we returned to process around the church building, the thick darkness defeated by waves of glowing candles. Every bird for

miles around seemed to join our joyful chorus as we
sang at first light,

> Your resurrection, O Christ our Savior,
> The angels in heaven sing.
> Enable us on earth
> To glorify You in purity of heart.

In the months that followed we burned up the mails
and phone lines, sharing our experience with Episcopal
friends we had left behind, friends now discovering for
themselves the hidden treasure of Orthodoxy. One year
later we returned to Spokane for a momentous
chrismation service. On that night, led by now Father
Anthony Creech, over ninety percent of our former
parish came home to Orthodoxy. A few months later
they received the name of St. Nicholas Antiochian Orthodox Church.

When I carried our oldest granddaughter, Alesha,
into our church for the first time, she caught her breath
at its beauty. Today I enter with the same sense of awe,
of unspeakable gratitude. Pungent incense drifts around
me. Large, sand-filled brass bowls anchor dozens of
slender brown beeswax candles, each a flickering symbol of fervent prayer. Tears sting my eyes as I bend to
kiss the icon of my Lord, then His Holy Mother, and
tuck alongside it a bright yellow rose from our garden.
I find a place among the friends who have become our

extended family, and watch arriving children stand on tiptoe to plant a kiss upon the day's theme icon.

Always new, always the same, the majestic, ancient liturgy at once echoes and answers every cry of my soul, and I am lost in adoring worship for the Lord who has so loved me. With overflowing heart I listen for His voice. At last, I hear.

During her almost five years as a student at Stanford University's School of Nursing, Mary squeezed in one creative writing class. "Train yourself to earn a living," her wise father counseled her. "If you have anything to say, you'll say it." She did both. The author of three books and more than five dozen articles and short stories, she views her chapter in this book as one of the most important contributions of her life. Mary and her husband Bob, parents of four and grandparents of seven, live in Marysville, Washington. They worship with their beloved church family at St. Paul Orthodox Church in Brier.

Suggestions for Further Reading

More Conversion Stories

Becoming Orthodox
by Fr. Peter Gillquist (Conciliar Press)
The story of the Evangelical Orthodox Church and its pilgrimage
to canonical Orthodoxy.

Anglican-Orthodox Pilgrimage
edited by Franklin Billerbeck (Conciliar Press)
Testimonies of Anglicans who have converted to Orthodoxy.

Coming Home
edited by Fr. Peter Gillquist (Conciliar Press)
Testimonies of Protestant clergymen of various denominations
who have converted to Orthodoxy.

Discovering the Rich Heritage of Orthodoxy
by Fr. Charles Bell (Light & Life Publishing)
Fr. Charles, a convert from the Presbyterian Church by way of the
charismatic Vineyard Movement, chronicles his journey to Orthodoxy and gives an easily accessible introduction to the Orthodox
Faith.

About the Orthodox Church

What Is the Orthodox Church?
by Fr. Marc Dunaway (Conciliar Press)
A brief overview of the history of the Orthodox Church.

Orthodoxy and Catholicism
by Fr. Theodore Pulcini (Conciliar Press)
A concise exposition of the differences between the Orthodox and
Roman Catholic faiths.

Apostolic Succession
by Fr. Gregory Rogers (Conciliar Press)
A well-researched overview of the doctrine of apostolic succession and its importance in the Church today.

Introducing the Orthodox Church
by Fr. Anthony Coniaris (Light & Life Publishing)
A complete but easy-to-read introduction to the doctrine and practice of the Orthodox Church.

The Orthodox Church
by Timothy (Bishop Kallistos) Ware (Penguin Books)
The classic, comprehensive work on the history of the Orthodox Church. Includes an explanation of the often-confusing relationship of the various Orthodox jurisdictions in America.

The Orthodox Faith
by Fr. Thomas Hopko (Orthodox Christian Publication Center)
A complete catechism in four easy-to-read volumes: Doctrine, Worship, Bible & Church History, and Spirituality.

The Orthodox Way
by Bishop Kallistos Ware (St. Vladimir's Seminary Press)
An introduction to Orthodox spirituality—theology as a way of life for the follower of Christ.

Periodicals

AGAIN Magazine (Conciliar Press)
A quarterly magazine calling America back to its roots in historic Orthodoxy once again.

The Handmaiden (Conciliar Press)
A quarterly journal offering support, encouragement, spiritual teaching, and appropriate role models for women serving God within the Orthodox Tradition.

All publications listed, and many more, are available through Conciliar Press. Write for a free catalog to Conciliar Press, P.O. Box 76, Ben Lomond, CA 95005, or call (800) 967-7377.